Basic Business Studies   Swift and Stanwell

English in the Office

Book 1 For Clerk-Typists and Transcribers

Sheila T Stanwell MInstAM FSCT
London University Teacher's Certificate
RSA TESFL Certificate with Distinction
Business Education Adviser
Ministry of Education, Jordan
formerly with United Nations and ILO

Moira K Swift LLB
Barrister-at-Law of Gray's Inn
formerly Principal Lecturer
Philippa Fawcett College

Edward Arnold

© S. T. Stanwell and M. K. Swift 1975

First published 1966
by Edward Arnold (Publishers) Ltd.,
25 Hill Street, London WIX 8LL

Reprinted 1966, 1969, 1970, 1972

Second edition 1975

ISBN: 0 7131 0001 X

The full course comprises:

Commerce (4th Edition)
Office Practice (3rd Edition)
English in the Office
Clerical Duties (3rd Edition)
International Trading
The Structure of Business
Retail Distribution
Office Practice Assignments
1001 Exercises
1001 Answers
Spirit Master Documents

The following Supplements are also available:

S1 Electronic Banking
S2 Law and Business: Recent Legislation
S3 Understanding the Financial Section of Your Newspaper (2E)
S4 Government Departments, Local Authorities and their Functions (2E)
S5 Commerce and the State (2E)

All rights reserved. No part of this publication may be reproduced, stored in a retrieval system, or transmitted in any form or by any means, electronic, mechanical, photocopying, recording or otherwise, without the prior permission of Edward Arnold (Publishers) Ltd.

Text set in 10/11 pt. Photon Baskerville, printed by photolithography and bound in Great Britain at The Pitman Press, Bath

Preface to the Course

English in the Office was originally published in 1966 as a single volume. It included information and exercises in those aspects of language, e.g. spelling and punctuation, which are important for transcribers; it also taught the application of the skills of composition and summarising to the work of secretaries; and it provided practice material for students preparing for the English Language examinations of leading examining bodies in commercial subjects.

In a preface of this nature written specifically for the informed reader, it is unnecessary to labour the point that since the first appearance of *English in the Office* there have been significant changes in the composition of commercial and secretarial courses, as regards both age and ability. Nowadays students range from CSE to post A-level, post-graduate and mature women on TOPS courses. All colleagues in the teaching profession will be aware of these changes. They will also know of changes in English Language examination papers—more questions requiring composition of some form or another, and fewer questions dealing with specific topics such as formation of plurals and insertion of punctuation marks. A third point of note is the increasing numbers of students who want to take up office work—both in this country and overseas—for whom English is a second or foreign language.

All these developments were borne in mind when we started to prepare the second edition, but despite them our original thinking still seemed valid, namely that the book served the needs of two groups (a) those who type and transcribe, and (b) those who compose. This consideration and the fact that book production costs are continually rising finally convinced us that it would be in everyone's interests to produce the new edition in separate parts, each book thereby being smaller, less expensive and written to serve specific needs.

Finally, it seemed that teachers working overseas or teaching commercial subjects in English as a second or foreign language, would need different classroom material from that contained in either of the first two parts. We, therefore, hope to complete the course, by producing a third book written for the special requirements of overseas and immigrant students.

The complete *English in the Office* course will comprise:

Book 1—For clerk-typists and transcribers

This book has been written to assist all those who transcribe—whether from conventional shorthand, abc shorthand, machine shorthand or recorded dictation—to produce perfect transcripts. The book does not prepare students for English examinations; its aim is to ensure that they do not fail audio- and shorthand-typewriting examinations because of English errors. Poor spelling, faulty punctuation and misuse of words, to name some of the commonest transcription errors, are caused by shortcomings in the skill of language.

Book 2—For secretaries

The aims of this book are to teach the application of the skills of summarising, comprehension, composition and communication to the work of secretaries. In compiling the contents the current English Language syllabuses of the main examining bodies have been borne in mind.

Book 3—For overseas students

This book aims to teach students of English as a second or foreign language the specialised vocabulary, expressions and style of English used in office work. Some remedial exercises will be included, but the emphasis will be on teaching the contemporary usage of office English, in both its spoken and written forms. In compiling the contents the current English for Overseas syllabuses of the main examinations have been borne in mind, particularly examinations in English for Commerce.

Fuller details regarding the aims, contents and suggestions for teachers will be given in the individual prefaces to each book.

Sheila T Stanwell
Moira K Swift
London, August 1974

Preface

This book has not been written to prepare students for English Language examinations; its aim is to ensure that they do not fail audio- and shorthand-typewriting examinations because of shortcomings in the use of language.

Colleagues who are familiar with the first edition of *English in the Office* will recognise that much of the old material has been retained. The chapters on punctuation, spelling, homophones, malapropisms, formation of plurals and the use of the dictionary have been updated and displayed in a style more relevant to the work of a typist; but the contents of these chapters have stood the test of time and have therefore been reprinted in almost their original form. The glossaries have been revised and updated.

The previous Chapter VI—Common Errors has been omitted entirely because, although specialists in Linguistics disagree on many issues, on one point there is almost universal agreement—that there is no such thing as good and bad in grammar*, what is correct means what is accepted as the correct usage by acknowledged authorities on the way English is used by educated native speakers at any given point in time and in any particular place. Language is continually developing and changing; although 'different from' is still thought of as being the more acceptable, 'different than' is gaining ground and may one day be the preferred form. Similarly with 'It's me!' and 'It's I!'—which of us caught unawares would instantaneously utter the latter rather than the former? It is, therefore, not easy to compile a list of deviations from standard usage which has universal and more than transient relevance. Teachers are quickly aware of any variations from the accepted norm which are common in the

---

* *Linguistics and Your Language*, R. A. Hall (Doubleday); *The Changing English Language*, Brian Foster (Penguin).

language usage of their students, and we feel that these variations are best dealt with by simple correction rather than by repetitive exercises.

A new chapter *Composing Simple Communications* has been added because the typist is frequently asked to write acknowledgments and covering letters from short verbal instructions. She therefore needs to know the basic requirements and layout of simple letters and memoranda.

All secretarial teachers will agree that the commonest transcription errors—faulty spelling, unacceptable punctuation and the misuse of words—are caused by an inadequate knowledge of English. The problem is a remedial one and the solving of it is more often than not the responsibility of the office skills teacher. We hope that teachers who are placed in this unenviable position will find the exercises and information presented in this book helpful for their students.

Sheila T Stanwell
Moira K Swift
London, August 1974

Acknowledgments

The authors are grateful to the Royal Society of Arts and to the London Chamber of Commerce for permission to reproduce and incorporate material from past examination papers into exercises at the ends of chapters; to Robert Hale Ltd. for permission to reproduce extracts from *Follow the Sun* by Jill Wordsworth; to *The Sunday Times* for permission to reproduce the poem on pages 32 and 33; to The Clarendon Press for two extracts from the *Concise Oxford Dictionary;* to Longmans, Green and Co. Ltd. for two extracts from *Roget's Thesaurus;* to W. and R. Chambers Ltd. for an extract from the *Shorter English Dictionary;* and to colleagues in the teaching profession and friends in commerce and industry for help and advice.

Contents

	Page
1 Punctuation	1

The purpose of punctuation. Paragraphs. Full stop—headings, contractions and abbreviations. Comma, colon and semicolon. The question mark and exclamation mark. The apostrophe. Quotation marks or inverted commas. Hyphen, dash, parentheses and brackets. Capital letters. Roman numerals. Typewriting conventions: leader dots, italics, footnotes. Exercises

2 Spelling   32

The difficulty of English spelling. Spelling rules. 'Trigger' words. 'Please yourself' words. Hints and suggestions. Spelling Lists. Exercises

3 Homophones   46

Definition. Why transcribers must pay special attention to homophones. Alphabetical lists and examples. Exercises

4 Words Easily Confused—Malapropisms   90

Definition. Why transcribers must pay special attention to Malapropisms. Alphabetical lists and examples. Exercises

5 Plurals   116

Formation. Agreement. Exercises

6 English Reference Books   121

The Dictionary—Arrangement, Pronunciation, Parts of Speech,

Meaning, Derivation, Plural Forms, Use of Capitals, Special Information, Usage, Idioms, Abbreviations. *Pitmans Shorthand/ English Dictionary. Good English. Modern English Usage. Usage and Abusage. Roget's Thesaurus. The Complete Plain Words. Deskbook of Correct English.* Exercises

7 Composing Simple Communications 131
Memoranda. Transmittal letters. Letters of confirmation. Acknowledgments. Exercises

Glossaries 144
1 Business Terms: Trading, Banking, Insurance 144
2 Meeting and Conference Terms 148
3 Abbreviations and Initials in Common Use 150
4 Foreign Words and Phrases in Common Use 156
5 Foreign Currencies 160
6 Roman Numerals 162

1

Punctuation

reference s s stroke m k s today's date to miss s smith six the vale newtown yorks postcode n e four two d b dear madam heading survey of number six the vale newtown yorks postcode n e four two d b block caps and underlined i have received your letter in which you invite me to make a survey of your property i understand that you propose to put the property on the market for sale in the early autumn i am very willing to undertake this survey for you but in view of the fact that there is still the best part of a year before you propose to sell your property i feel that it would be more in your interest if i made the survey a little later in the year so that there can be no chance of any major change in either the value of your property or in the surrounding neighbourhood there is so much development at present in your neighbourhood that each month sees a different set of circumstances which may or may not affect the value of properties you should not assume that this development will devaluate your property on the contrary the development of shopping centres such as that envisaged in your immediately adjacent suburb would add greatly to the value of your own site if on the other hand you wish to embody the possible purchase price of your property in calculations which have immediate significance then i shall of course carry out your wishes within the next few weeks i estimate that as the property is fairly extensive i shall require two days to complete the task i understand that part of the stabling and one wing of your house are let as separate dwellings and it will be necessary for me to have access to both these parts of the main structure if i am to give a complete report it will also be necessary for me to be able to examine the floor boards under any fitted carpets and in cupboards perhaps you will facilitate this when you reply i shall be glad if you will let me know if there are any dates within the next three weeks which would be preferable to you yours faithfully john brown and sons surveyors and valuers

You would be very surprised to receive a letter looking like this. Why? Is it because it has no paragraphs?

Here it is divided into paragraphs.

reference s s stroke m k s

today's date

to miss s smith six the vale newtown yorks n e four two d b

dear madam

heading survey of number six the vale newtown yorks n e four two d b block caps and underlined

i have received your letter in which you invite me to make a survey of your property i understand that you propose to put the property on the market for sale in the early autumn

i am very willing to undertake this survey for you but in view of the fact that there is still the best part of a year before you propose to sell your property i feel that it would be more in your interest if i made the survey a little later in the year so that there can be no chance of any major change in either the value of your property or in the surrounding neighbourhood there is so much development at present in your neighbourhood that each month sees a different set of circumstances which may or may not affect the value of properties you should not assume that this development will devaluate your property on the contrary the development of shopping centres such as that envisaged in your immediately adjacent suburb would add greatly to the value of your own site

if on the other hand you wish to embody the possible purchase price of your property in calculations which have immediate significance then i shall of course carry out your wishes within the next few weeks i estimate that as the property is fairly extensive i shall require two days to complete the task

i understand that part of the stabling and one wing of your house are let as separate dwellings and it will be necessary for me to have access to both these parts of the main structure if i am to give a complete report it will also be necessary for me to be able to examine the floorboards under any fitted carpets and in cupboards perhaps you will facilitate this when you reply i shall be glad if you will let me know if there are any dates within the next three weeks which would be preferable to you

yours faithfully

john brown and sons
surveyors and valuers

Even with paragraphs it does not look as you would expect, because it has no capital letters and no punctuation. It is interesting to note that modern business practice has moved towards this layout, with all lines starting at the lefthand margin, and as little punctuation as possible.

Here is the same letter broken into sentences and divided only by full stops. Capital letters have been put in where necessary.

SS/MKS   30 August 1975

Miss S Smith
6 The Vale
NEWTOWN Yorks
NE4 2DB

Dear Madam

SURVEY OF 6 THE VALE NEWTOWN YORKS NE4 2DB

I have received your letter in which you invite me to make a survey of your property. I understand that you propose to put the property on the market for sale in the early autumn.

I am very willing to undertake this survey for you but in view of the fact that there is still the best part of a year before you propose to sell your property I feel that it would be more in your interest if I made the survey a little later in the year so that there can be no chance of any major change in either the value of your property or in the surrounding neighbourhood. There is so much development at present in your neighbourhood that each month sees a different set of circumstances which may or may not affect the value of properties. You should not assume that this development will devaluate your property. On the contrary the development of shopping centres such as that envisaged in your immediately adjacent suburb would add greatly to the value of your own site.

If on the other hand you wish to embody the possible purchase price of your property in calculations which have immediate significance then I shall of course carry out your wishes within the next few weeks. I estimate that as the property is fairly extensive I shall require two days to complete the task.

I understand that part of the stabling and one wing of your house are let as separate dwellings and it will be necessary for me to have access to both these parts of the main structure if I am to give a complete report. It will also be necessary for me to be able to examine the floor boards under any fitted carpets and in cupboards. Perhaps you will facilitate this.

When you reply I shall be glad if you will let me know if there are any days within the next three weeks which would be preferable to you.

Yours faithfully

John Brown and Sons
Surveyors and Valuers

When you read this through you will probably understand it quite well but it may make you feel a bit breathless. Why? Is it because there aren't any commas? On the next page the same letter appears with additional punctuation. It has been typed in the style known as semi-indented; this

3

style was fashionable until a few years ago. Nowadays the full-block style with open punctuation (i.e. no punctuation before or after the body of the letter) shown on page 3 is most commonly used.

SS/MKS   30 August 1975

Miss S Smith
6 The Vale
NEWTOWN Yorks
NE4 2DB

Dear Madam

                SURVEY OF 6 THE VALE NEWTOWN YORKS NE4 2DB

    I have received your letter in which you invite me to make a survey of your property. I understand that you propose to put the property on the market for sale in the early autumn.

    I am very willing to undertake this survey for you but, in view of the fact that there is still the best part of a year before you propose to sell your property, I feel that it would be more in your interest if I made the survey a little later in the year so that there can be no chance of any major change, in either the value of your property or in the surrounding neighbourhood. There is so much development at present in your neighbourhood that each month sees a different set of circumstances, which may or may not affect the value of properties. You should not assume that this development will devaluate your property. On the contrary, the development of shopping centres such as that envisaged in your immediately adjacent suburb would add greatly to the value of your own site.

    If, on the other hand, you wish to embody the possible purchase price of your property in calculations which have immediate significance, then I shall, of course, carry out your wishes within the next few weeks. I estimate that, as the property is fairly extensive, I shall require two days to complete the task.

    I understand that part of the stabling and one wing of your house are let as separate dwellings, and it will be necessary for me to have access to both these parts of the main structure if I am to give a complete report. It will also be necessary for me to be able to examine the floor boards under any fitted carpets and in cupboards. Perhaps you will facilitate this.

    When you reply I shall be glad if you will let me know if there are any days within the next three weeks which would be preferable to you than others.

                            Yours faithfully

                            John Brown and Sons
                            Surveyors and Valuers

Here is the letter displayed in the semi-indented style. Although the body of the letter is punctuated in the conventional way, the open* style has

   * Explanations and definitions of *open* and *close* punctuation are given in *You Have a Point There,* by Eric Partridge (pub. Hamish Hamilton).

been retained for the inside address, the salutation and the complimentary close.

Look at the examples of letters which come before this page. It is probable, with imagination, that you could understand the second and third examples but not the example on page 1. The ridiculous appearance of the letter in the first illustration makes a very strong case for knowing and understanding the correct use of punctuation. It is the same strong case which can be made for speech which is clear, which has helpful pauses and emphasis, is interesting and has purposeful intonation. The business of giving and receiving communication forms the topic of a later chapter in this book, but in this, the first chapter, we deal with one of the most important aspects of the use of written English. The reason is simple.

When you sit at a typewriter to transcribe from notes, you are turning shorthand, or other written or printed notes, into English prose. If you are transcribing from sound, you have an even greater responsibility, since you have not had the opportunity, at the time when the notes were dictated, of asking any questions about things which may have been difficult to understand.

Sometimes, notes which may be difficult to read, or sounds which may be difficult to hear, make you feel that the dictated matter does not make sense. Here you have only one rule to follow. You *cannot, in any circumstances whatsoever, type what you know, or even suspect is not sense*. What you type *must* make sense, and what is more, it must consist of well-constructed sentences and paragraphs, with the proper use of punctuation. If punctuation is not properly used, the sense of a sentence may be altered. Some people, when dictating, give the punctuation they want; others do not. If they do not, you must put it in, and therefore you must understand it very well indeed.

This chapter is written to show you how to use punctuation and how to become so accustomed to its use that to punctuate becomes a habit with you, and does not cause you great difficulty.

Paragraphs

When you read through your shorthand notes before transcribing them the first thing you should do is to mark off the paragraphs. If you compare the first two examples in this chapter you will find that the division into paragraphs of the second example helped to make the letter easier to understand. Generally speaking, you should start a new paragraph whenever a new topic is introduced. Each paragraph is a self-contained unit which makes a positive contribution to the theme of the whole letter.

If you are typing a dialogue, begin a new paragraph for each speaker. This enables the reader to follow the conversation and avoids jarring the narrative by the frequent use of 'he said', 'she said'.

```
            "Ah!" he said.  "Here is the lady and here is the pilot.
    Are you ready to start at once?"

            "No," I said, "my things are up at the hotel."

            "Have you any transport?"

            "No."

            "Then I had better run you up.  How long will it take
    you to collect your things?"

            "Five minutes."  I didn't add that this included
    packing.

            We got into a red jeep and tore up the hill.*
```

Full stop

The stop that comes at the end of a sentence is called a full stop or period. It is the one punctuation mark that cannot be done away with, and most people, even those who claim not to understand how to punctuate, feel they must use full stops. The reason is that when people speak they cannot go on without stopping now and then to take breath, and this automatically breaks up what they say into clearly marked divisions. The pause ends a thought or closes an argument. In the same way the full stop ends a train of thought.

Headings—Full stops are unnecessary in all titles of books, articles, compositions and similar headings.

Contractions and abbreviations—H W Fowler in *Modern English Usage* recommends leaving out the full stop from words such as *Mr* and *Mrs* when the contraction ends with the same letter as the uncontracted form: *Mr* instead of *Mr.*, *hr* instead of *hr.*, *yd* instead of *yd.*, and so on. This can also be done with such terms as *min, lb, oz* and with the contracted forms in common use for initials, degrees, honours, offices, etc. Therefore, it is acceptable to type:

```
                    A B Smith Esq DSO MC MA
```

and BBC, BR, UNESCO, HMSO.

Even where a contracted term forms an unabbreviated word, *number*—*no*, *inch*—*in*, the full stop can be left out as the context usually shows the meaning.†

These recommendations have not yet been universally adopted and many people still use the full stops in names, degrees and the other examples set out above.

* Extract from *Follow the Sun* by Jill Wordsworth (Robert Hale Ltd.).
† This principle has been adopted by the British Standards Institution.

Abbreviations for the names of units and the plurals of contracted arithmetical terms should be written without a full stop. Study the following examples:

3rd	A4
75 cwt	10 kg
4 mm	5 in
6 cm	10 kW
50 km	65p

Commas

There are some sentences, even long and complex ones, which need no punctuation other than a full stop. But most sentences do require punctuating with other punctuation marks, in order to separate the main thought from other subsidiary or descriptive thoughts, or to show a change of subject.

The most usual way to break up a sentence is by way of commas. A comma may be used between words, word-groups, phrases, and between the principal part of the sentence and clauses, or clauses and other clauses. When you read this you may feel that you do not know what is meant by 'principal part of a sentence' or 'a clause'. We must then go further back and begin by thinking of what is meant by a sentence.

Every sentence, even a very long one, has certainly two, and probably, three, parts.

1. It has a person or a thing which says or does something, or has something done to him, her or it.
2. It has a word, called a verb, which describes what is done.
3. Sometimes it has a person or thing which is linked to the verb directly.
4. Sometimes, rather more indirectly, there are words which show to whom, or by whom or what, 'something' is done.

In some sentences you will find examples of both (3) and (4) above. Look at these sentences broken up and numbered with the divisions 1, 2, 3 and 4:

1	2	3	4
Jim	sailed		
Jim	sailed	the boat	
Jim	sailed	the boat	on the lake
Mary	was hit		by the car
Mary	was hit		on the head by the car

It is possible to put in descriptions, either one word (adjectives or adverbs) or a group of words (clauses or phrases) to describe any part of the sentences already written. Look at this chart. The descriptions are printed in italic type.

1	2	3	4
Jim		the boat	on the lake *in the park*
	proudly	*which was a*	
who was	sailed	*birthday*	
six today		*present*	

Here it is, written straight out, with the descriptive parts still printed in different type:

Jim *who was six today* proudly sailed the boat *which was a birthday present* on the lake *in the park*.

Is there any place in this sentence where you feel a break, a comma, is necessary? The tendency is to use as few commas as possible. The comma today either causes a pause, as in speech, or, more often, is necessary because it shows the construction of the sentence. The sentence above could be written:

Jim, who was six today, proudly sailed the boat, which was a birthday present, on the lake in the park.

Here the commas are separating the descriptive words, which were hitherto printed in a different type from the principal part of the sentence. You will notice that there is not a comma after 'lake' and this is because the words 'in the park' are doing the work of an adjective or a word describing the lake such as 'the round lake' whereas the other parts are like little sentences each having a (1) and (2) as above. These groups of words each with its own noun and verb are known as clauses, whereas the words 'in the park' (*without* a verb) are known as a phrase. It is quite possible, however, that today you might well see the sentence written:

Jim who was six today sailed the boat which was a birthday present, on the lake in the park.

You will notice that *one* comma has been retained. Why? Because without it the words 'on the lake in the park' relate to the last noun (person or thing) mentioned, in this case the birthday present, which is certainly not what you or the writer meant.

If, however, you alter the order of the groups of words, then the commas become necessary. Look at:

On the lake in the park Jim who was six today sailed his boat which was a birthday present.

The commas are necessary:

On the lake in the park, Jim, who was six today, sailed his boat, which was a birthday present.

Here then is the first obvious use of a comma. It is to separate from a word or group of words another word or group of words, which, if left joined, would mean something different. This also applies when the comma is used to separate words which, when joined by *and* do not usually need a comma. Look at the following sets of sentences which, if left without commas as on the right, mean something different from the sentences on the left.

1. He himself took the letter to the minister, following normal routine.

   (Here he follows normal routine)

   He himself took the letter to the minister following normal routine.

   (Here the minister is the one who follows normal routine)

2. He avoided the girl, knowing the circumstances of the case.

   (Here he avoided the girl because he knew the circumstances)

   He avoided the girl knowing the circumstances of the case.

   (Here he avoided the particular girl who knew the circumstances)

3. This course is for men, transferring to other departments, to qualify for promotion.

   (This describes the men on the course)

   This course is for men, transferring to other departments to qualify for promotion.

   (This also describes the men but indicates that the purpose of their transfer is to qualify for promotion)

It would be possible to write a very long list of such examples, but to avoid them, rules are necessary and we have set out here the very minimum of rules for the use of commas.

1 A comma is used instead of the word *and* between nouns, pronouns, adjectives, verbs and adverbs. Here is one example of each. If you find it difficult to recognise a noun, etc., perhaps this will help you.

Nouns	The violin, the viola and the double bass are string instruments.
	The violin, the viola, the double bass are string instruments.
Adjectives	She was a thin, sad and pathetic figure.
	She was a thin, sad, pathetic figure.
Verbs	She ran, slipped and fell.
	She ran, slipped, fell.
Adverbs	She sat sadly, silently and patiently.
	She sat sadly, silently, patiently.

2 A comma is used between single words and phrases, and between phrases and phrases (treating the phrases exactly as if they were single words) as above, because the phrases are doing the job of a noun, adjective, verb or adverb.

(a) John, looking very self-conscious, slipped out.

Here the phrase *looking very self-conscious* does the work of an adjective and describes John.

(b) John walked, without a glance behind him, until he reached Mary.

Here the phrase *without a glance behind him* does the work of an adverb and describes the way John walked.

(c) John walked, without a glance behind him, until he reached Mary, who, hidden by some desks, did not see him approaching.

Here the phrase *hidden by some desks* describes Mary.

3 Commas between principal and subordinate clauses. When the important (principal) part comes first, there is no need for a comma.

He looked at the television because he had finished his homework.

But if you reverse the order then you must use a comma.

Because he had finished his homework, he looked at the television.

Again:

His father promised him a watch when he passed his advanced level exams.

When he passed his advanced level exams, his father promised him a watch.

4 Commas are used to separate one subordinate clause from another if more than one occur in a sentence. This is unusual.

When you come to be interested in punctuation, if ever you do, you will find your transcription more interesting too.

5 In very complex sentences, commas separate words from words, words from groups of words or clauses, and principal clauses (important parts) from other important parts.

If, when you have read this chapter, you feel you understand better, or at least a little better, the use of punctuation, then we shall feel that our efforts, for what they are worth, were not made in vain.

One word of warning. There are certain groups of words (known as adjectival clauses) which describe things. If these words do not suggest a restriction a comma is necessary, before and after the words. If they *do* suggest a restriction then a comma is not necessary. Look at:

The barrister, who was acting for the accused person, agreed to the appeal.

Shakespearean plays, presented in modern dress, provide a refreshing study.

but

A book which is cheap and readily obtainable by all students is urgently needed.

Shakespearean plays presented in modern dress provide an interesting study, but those presented in traditional historical dress are a larger box-office attraction.

6 In addresses, figures, dates, etc. the use of the comma is disappearing. If you ignore this modern trend, a comma is used at the end of the name, and each part of an address. Compare

Miss Mary Smith, 14 Chapell Street, WILMSLOW, Cheshire, WM3 6DR	with	Miss Mary Smith 14 Chapell Street WILMSLOW Cheshire WM3 6DR

Notice there is no comma after 14 in either example. In both examples the post-town is typed in block capitals as requested by the British Post Office Corporation.

In dates, if commas are used they are used only after the day and/or month:

> Thursday, 14th March, 1975.

The current feeling is to leave them out, just as the full stop has disappeared from the end of the date, and write simply:

> 14 March 1975

Colons and semicolons

The full stop is the longest pause. There are other punctuation pauses which can be fairly long, but not so definite in bringing to an end a particular line of thought. They act as stop-gaps. They are the colon and the semicolon.

The **colon** is an introductory piece of punctuation. You probably know it as this when you see it used before a list of things, or in an examination paper—'Write short notes on the following:'

In just the same way, when it is used in a sentence it is introductory to the part of the sentence following it. Look at this sentence:

> We have written this chapter to help you with your transcription: but first you must learn the rules of punctuation.

You can also use a colon where you leave out a word normally used to join parts of the sentence, for instance 'but':

> You may find these rules very difficult at first: (but) everyone does.

Or, where you are deliberately drawing, in the second part of the sentence, a conclusion from what you have said in the first part:

You are a secretary: as such you are very much in demand.

Or where you have a second thought:

We have written this book for transcribers and we think it will help them: their greatest help, however, is the accumulation of their experience.

Colons are also used in lists such as contents of chapters on the *Contents* pages of books.

A **semicolon** does less than a colon. It is stronger than a comma but weaker than a colon. It interrupts, but it does not end a thought or sentence. It merely emphasises or separates a clause from the words surrounding it. A semicolon can be used in many instances where we have suggested a comma be used, but most usefully semicolons are employed when one wants to separate independent clauses without using a conjunction, as for instance:

Mary has neglected to practise her shorthand speed and (conjunction) eventually her shorthand will become useless.

Mary has neglected to practise her shorthand speed; eventually her shorthand will become useless.

Sometimes it is possible to use full stops or commas instead of semicolons, but in the following type of sentence the semicolon is preferable. Even a colon would not be wrong:

At first she did not like the sound of the job and refused it; when she had thought it over, however, she saw she was wrong and accepted the post.

Semicolons are useful in lists which form part of a sentence:

Two; four; six; eight; the increasing size of the groups became evident to the onlookers.

Besides the main punctuation marks which help to clarify sentences, you must know how to use quotation marks or inverted commas, apostrophes, the question mark and exclamation mark, hyphen, dash and parentheses.

Question Mark

The **question mark** is also known as the interrogation mark. It is used at the end of a direct question.

'Where are you going?' she asked.
Do you think the building will be ready by the end of June?

Do not use a question mark after an indirect question such as:

She asked me where I was going.

Or after a request, although this may be disguised as a question:

> Will you please send me a copy of your new catalogue.

Exclamation Mark

The **exclamation mark** is used after commands, wishes disguised as commands and exclamations.

> Go out of the room!
> I wish you'd stop doing that!
> Ugh! What a horrible sight!

Apostrophe

The **apostrophe** has three uses; firstly to show possession, secondly to show omission and thirdly to form the plural of letters and figures.

(1) to show possession:

Singular nouns add *'s* to show possession:

Singular	*Possession*
The boy	The boy's book
The lady	The lady's house
The company	The company's directors
The baby	The baby's rattle
Henry	Henry's car
The man	The man's suitcase

Plural nouns add only the apostrophe to show possession:

Plural	*Possession*
The boys	The boys' school
The ladies	The ladies' cloakroom
The companies	The companies' directors
The babies	The babies' playroom

EXCEPT when the plural form does not end in *s*. The commonest of these words are *men, women* and *children*. To form the possessive of these words, simply add *'s*.

Plural	*Possession*
The men	The men's lockers
The women	The women's meeting
The children	The children's programme

(2) to show omission. The apostrophe takes the place of the missing letter:

is not—isn't	did not—didn't	they are—they're
it is—it's	I have—I've	could not—couldn't

(3) To form the plural of single letters and figures *'s* is used to avoid confusion:

> Do you spell your name with two t's?
> There are two m's in accommodate.
> 'I've got three 6's!' he exclaimed.

Time phrases. Formerly time phrases such as *in a year's time, a two hours' delay, three weeks' holiday* used the apostrophe. Modern usage, however, discourages this practice.

Similarly the plural forms of abbreviations may also be written without the apostrophe: M.A.s, M.P.s. The apostrophe should, however, be retained in such phrases as *at the grocer's, one o'clock, for goodness' sake, for Heaven's sake, my heart's desire.*

S-S type words. Words ending in two *s* sounds, like *Moses* and *hostesses*, should not have a third *s* sound added. Therefore, to form the possessives of these and similar words, only the apostrophe is added.

Moses	Moses'			St. James	St. James's
hostesses	hostesses'	}	*but* {	hostess	hostess's
Jesus	Jesus'			Chambers	Chambers's

Princess's breaks this rule but has become accepted usage.

Quotation marks or inverted commas

There are two types of these called commonly *single quotes* and *double quotes*. Today single quotes are becoming increasingly used.

> 'The sentence "The quick brown fox jumped over the lazy dog" is familiar to most typists.'

The position of the punctuation is explained if the quote is moved to the end of the sentence:

> 'Most typists are familiar with the sentence "The quick brown fox jumped over the lazy dog".'

If a further element of conversation is introduced, the inverted commas used as quotation marks recur each time there is a change from direct to indirect speech. In the following sentences the direct speech is printed in italics:

> He said, *'Most typists are familiar with the sentence "The quick brown fox jumped over the lazy dog",'* but he added, *'few typists are aware of the reason for their being asked to type this "finger-twister".'*

Notice the position of the comma and the full stop. If single quotes are preferred (and this is often the case today) the reverse arrangement is made:

> He said, *'Most typists are familiar with the sentence "The quick brown fox*

jumped over the lazy dog",,' but he added, *'few typists are aware of the reason for their being asked to type this "finger-twister".'*

If the quotation or direct speech has by any chance to be put in a bracket then the bracket remains *outside* everything, and the period (or comma) comes inside the inverted commas, *inside* the brackets.

(His employer said, 'This is the person I want you to meet.')

Hyphens

Hyphens are used to separate what are known as compound words. Such words are usually adjectives (descriptive words) or nouns (names of people and things):

> Many well-known people attended the demonstration of the vertical take-off plane.

Hyphens are used to separate numbers from twenty to ninety-nine—twenty-one, thirty-one, forty-one, etc.

In *Modern English Usage* Fowler introduces his article on the hyphen with the remark, 'The chaos prevailing among writers or printers or both regarding the use of hyphens is discreditable to English education.' The confusion regarding the use of the hyphen may be illustrated from *The Scottish Pupil's Spelling Book* where 'ice cream, ice-cream, icecream' all are given as forms being in common use.

The use of the hyphen should be eliminated as far as possible and the spelling of compound words as one word is far better; if this is unsuitable, two words without a hyphen should be used.

With some prefixes a hyphen is necessary to avoid confusion:

> anti-freeze, pre-election, semi-absorbent

Pay careful attention to the following:

> bathroom   dining-room
> bedroom   sitting-room

The dash

The dash, used before and after a word or group of words, is used to isolate that word or group of words in a way that the four main punctuation marks, the full stop, colon, semicolon and comma are unable to do. It can be used within a sentence sometimes where a comma would be used and sometimes deliberately to put in a parenthesis (an aside) where a comma could not be used.

It is true to say that even when you are an experienced transcriber it would be difficult to describe when you would use a dash: it is a matter of 'feel'. Apart from being used to emphasise what you might otherwise have put between commas, it is used to interrupt, to bring to an abrupt end or to add an afterthought. The following are examples of the use of the dash. You will see that in some cases two dashes are necessary, in other cases only one.

Instead of commas

He said—and I heard him quite clearly—that I was fool.

The students—and there were nearly a hundred of them present—were unanimous in their praise of their tutor.

To interrupt

He was highly successful—but we have said that before.

There he goes. He should have been great, but alas—well, you know him.

To bring to an abrupt end or add an afterthought

Of course you can have it—it is yours, anyway.
He is always here on time—when he is sober.

Non-punctuational

The dash is also used, but *not* as a means of punctuation, to indicate letters left out or to add the name of an author or source of information.

Go to H—and leave me alone.
Mr. J— B— is a dashing young man.
To be or not to be—Shakespeare.

Special note for typists

If you study this page you will see that the printer uses one sign for the hyphen and a longer sign for the dash. It is very easy to distinguish one from the other. But the typewriter has only one sign – usually a lower case character on the same key as the righthand bracket. The typist distinguishes the hyphen from the bracket by leaving one clear space each side of the hyphen key when it stands for a bracket. Compare

```
       pre-election      dining-room     1975-6     Director-General
```
WITH
```
       He said - and I heard him quite clearly - that I was a fool.
```

A hyphen connects or joins together.
A dash divides or separates.

Parentheses between brackets

A parenthesis is a group of words which are not necessary to the sense of the sentence. The sentence, and the sense, is quite complete, quite clear without the parenthesis. The words forming a parenthesis either explain, comment upon, add to, or refer to, what has already been said or is being said.

We have met two cases of such words or groups of words before. These are firstly groups of words placed between commas, such as: 'Mary, a born rebel, did not care what people thought about her appearance,' and secondly, words placed between dashes: 'Mary—a born rebel—did not care what people thought about her appearance.' The third way to indicate a parenthesis is to place the words in brackets, and in this case the words are rendered even less important to the true meaning of the sentence. They are an 'insertion'. If the other words do not make sense without them, then they are not truly a parenthesis, and should not be placed between brackets, but between commas. It is wise to try to avoid using brackets if possible.

Here are some examples of parentheses:

Mary went to St. Francis' School (a secondary modern school) which was six miles from her home.

In this series of books (Basic Business Studies) the authors have tried to write in a simple style.

His error (involving many vehicles) caused a delay of many hours.

Mr. Levy, the Chairman, then read his report (this had previously been circulated to members) and answered questions about its content.

Use of capital letters

There is at least one simple rule. You must always use a capital letter when you have finished the previous words with a full stop, question mark or exclamation mark:

We have written a text book. We hope you find it useful.

Do you know we have written a text book? We hope you find it useful.

You really didn't know we had written a text book! We thought everyone knew.

After this the rules are not quite so straightforward but they can be simplified to some extent. All the following require capitalisation:

1 Names of people and places.

John lives in England.
Fouad lives in Jordan.

2 When a word describing a relative such as father or mother is used instead of that relative's name. Hence, we write:

Dear Father
I said to Father

but

I said to my father

Nicknames and pet names also take a capital.

3 All words describing a deity:

> God,
> The Father, the Son and the Holy Ghost,

and this rule includes the pronouns and other references to deities:

> Jesus Christ so loved the world that He gave His only begotten Son.
> Praise be to Allah, Who is the Prophet.

4 The days of the week and the months of the year, but not seasons, except in poetry.

5 Acts of Parliament, Bills, and the names and titles of judges, peers, officials, churchmen and other dignitaries:

> Contracts of Employment Act, 1972
> Equal Pay Act, 1970
> Finance Act, 1974
> His Honour Judge Jeffries
> Mr. Justice Devlin
> The Duke of Bedford
> The Bishop of Willesden

6 The names of ships:

> S.S. Queen Elizabeth.

7 Trade names, legal documents (to avoid confusion), the armed services and units of the services, official bodies, the stars and planets:

> Rolls Royce engines are famous throughout the world.
> He discussed his Will with his solicitor.

or

> He discussed the Deed with his solicitor.

(Note that if capitals are not used there is a quite different meaning.)

> The march included men of the Royal Navy, the Army and the Royal Air Force.
> The National Coal Board.
> It has now become possible to reach Mars.

8 Technical use of ordinary words:

> The Crown is liable for the torts of its servants.
> The Burmese Cat is now an established breed in this country.
> A Common Noun does not demand capitalisation.
> Teacher Training is being stepped up.
> The Inns of Court contain many beautiful features.

9 Literary use of capital letters.

Book titles and quotations require the use of capital letters:

Have you read Basic Business Studies, Book 1?

10 The first word of direct speech even if it is preceded by punctuation other than a full stop:

She asked, 'Have you now come to the end?'

but

'Have you,' she asked, 'now come to the end?'

Numbers

Here are some principles to help you decide whether to write numbers in figures or words:

1 In general work numbers under ten should be written out.

I shall be away from the office for the next two days.

2 Use figures for numbers over ten except when they open a sentence.

We have received 67 crates of china.
Thirty-six members attended the meeting.

3 Use figures with *a.m.* and *p.m.* and words with *o'clock*.

The train arrives at 6.25 p.m.
The meeting starts at six o'clock.

4 Approximations and indefinite numbers should be written in words:

There are about a thousand students in the school.
Approximately three hundred members attended the meeting.

5 Use figures for dates, addresses, numbered lists, scores in games and matches and after the abbreviation No.

Roman numerals

You have probably seen Roman numerals on memorial and foundation stones and used them in history for titles of kings, e.g. Henry V. Roman numerals are used in literary work and business documents and reports for:

1 Numbering chapters and headings.
2 Enumerating sections or paragraphs of schedules and reports.
3 Enumerating appendices.

Small Roman numerals are used for numbering pages in prefaces and for sub-paragraphs (i, ii, iii, iv, v, and so on).

1	I	6	VI	50	L	6,000	$\overline{\text{VI}}$
2	II	7	VII	100	C	1,000,000	$\overline{\text{M}}$
3	III	8	VIII	500	D	(The overscore multiplies	
4	IV	9	IX	1,000	M	the number by 1,000)	
5	V	10	X				

To work out Roman numerals take each figure by itself:

16 = 10 + 6 = X + VI = XVI
19 = 10 + 9 = X + IX = XIX
30 = XXX
40 = XL
49 = 40 + 9 = XL + IX = XLIX

99 = 90 + 9 = XC + IX = XCIX
543 = 500 + 40 + 3 = D + XL + III
      = DXLIII
1965 = 1,000 + 900 + 60 + 5 = M
    + CM + LX + V = MCMLXV

Typewriting conventions

Typewriting examining bodies and professional associations have established a number of conventions regarding punctuation. These are frequently at variance with suggestions put forward by specialists in English punctuation. They have been summarised here under the heading *Typewriting Conventions* so that you will know they are not considered in quite the same light as the main punctuation marks.

Leader dots are groups of full stops, used in tables, lists, etc., to lead the eye across a space to the right word or number. Thus:

    ..   ..   (two full stops, three spaces)
    . . . . .   (one full stop, two spaces)
    ... ... (three full stops, two spaces)

Italics. Italic printing is different from ordinary print in that it is lighter and slopes to the right. Italic letters are used to distinguish words and sentences for emphasis (It is *too* hot!), for titles of newspapers and magazines (I read it in *The Times*), for foreign words and phrases (The matter is still *sub judice*) and for words used as examples, as you will see throughout this book.

To indicate italic print in typewritten matter, use the underscore.

Footnotes. You will find several examples of footnotes in this book. Information additional to the main text but nevertheless relevant may be brought to the reader's attention by using a footnote. Typists indicate these by using an asterisk (x and hyphen, thus x), a dagger (I and hyphen, thus I), or double dagger (I and equals sign, thus ╪); these signs attempt to imitate printers' signs, like the following

                •   †   ‡

EXERCISES

1. Type or write the following sentences inserting the apostrophe where necessary:
   (a) There isnt any news.
   (b) We couldnt go to Marys party.
   (c) The dogs lost its collar.
   (d) Wheres the new secretarys office?
   (e) The secretaries training course begins at ten oclock on Monday.
   (f) Staff may leave at 11.30 a.m. on Saturdays, subject to the exigencies of the Companys service.
   (g) The companies directors were appointed on 12th May, 1974.
   (h) Childrens clothes are cheaper this year.
   (i) Moses grave is at Nebi Musa near Jericho.
   (j) Two famous queens endowed Queens College.

2. Type or write the following sentences inserting the apostrophe where necessary:
   (a) The Ladies Night was well attended.
   (b) The directors agreed to the mens request.
   (c) A new boys school is to be built on that site.
   (d) Well see you at Pats on Sunday.
   (e) The offices are near Regents Park.
   (f) The companys moving to larger premises.
   (g) The companies discussed the formation of an employers federation.
   (h) Ill telephone the butchers and order the meat.
   (i) What do you think of our childrens books?

3. Type or write the following sentences inserting the apostrophe where necessary.
   (a) Our school is only a stones throw from the station.
   (b) Its very warm today.
   (c) Johns going to Franks for his holidays.
   (d) Theyre not sure whos going.
   (e) Please order six copies of Chamberss dictionary.
   (f) Has the cat had its dinner?
   (g) Whose books are these?
   (h) For goodness sake, dont make that mistake again.
   (i) The womens representatives will meet on Thursday afternoon.

4. Type or write the following sentences with the correct capitalisation:
   (a) The sales manager will visit the middle east in the spring.
   (b) The prime minister will return to london in time for the opening of parliament.
   (c) When he leaves school he will join either the army or the police.
   (d) They will travel to the united states on the queen mary.
   (e) He has made a will leaving everything to the royal heart foundation.
   (f) The duke of edinburgh is a popular member of the royal family.
   (g) I advise you to buy teach yourself french.

(h) What a lovely dress! where did you buy it?
   (i) I am going to the holy land for my holidays this year.
   (j) I have written to mother today.

5 Type or write the following sentences with correct capitalisation:
   (a) 'do you think', he said, 'the train will arrive on time?'
   (b) Their marriage has been arranged to take place at christmas.
   (c) We call my sister tiny as she is so small.
   (d) 'Have you visited rome? it is a beautiful city.'
   (e) Many people have opposed the rent bill.
   (f) 'Dear uncle, thanks very much for the cheque.'
   (g) The bishop of southwark conducted the service.
   (h) He has left the church of england and become a buddhist.
   (i) We shall be leaving for the far east in the autumn.
   (j) My father is an officer in the royal navy.

6 Type or write the following sentences inserting the hyphen where necessary:
   (a) He got into a first class carriage.
   (b) She looked into the blue green water of the lake.
   (c) Her daughter in law came to stay with her.
   (d) He has bought a second hand car.
   (e) Do not forget to put anti freeze in the car radiator.
   (f) My daughter will be twenty one in August.
   (g) The programme included many well loved ballads.
   (h) I have lost my umbrella; I must recover it.
   (i) It is difficult for semi skilled men to find work.
   (j) My umbrella is old; it must be recovered.

7 Type or write the following sentences inserting the hyphen where necessary:
   (a) There is a shortage of first class shorthand typists today.
   (b) She felt very self conscious when she entered the restaurant.
   (c) Many married women accept part time work.
   (d) Her husband is of Anglo French origin.
   (e) I hope to be home again by mid December.
   (f) My husband invited his co director to the party.
   (g) This time table is now non operative.
   (h) When I go to America I shall fly by Pan American.
   (i) The dining room of the house is very small.
   (j) Mr Brown will attend the staff meeting ex officio.

8 Write three sentences showing the use of each of the following punctuation marks:
   (a) full stop
   (b) colon
   (c) semicolon
   (d) comma
   (e) question mark
   (f) exclamation mark
   (g) inverted commas (single or double)
   (h) dash
   (i) brackets
   (j) apostrophe

9 Type or write the following sentences writing any figures in words where you think necessary:
 (a) He visited the office 2 days ago.
 (b) 10 minutes is a long time to wait.
 (c) We have sold 3,625 sets this month.
 (d) Their house has only 1 bathroom.
 (e) Only 6 people turned up for the choir practice.
 (f) It is nearly 200 years since the French Revolution.
 (g) There are approximately 30 children in each class.
 (h) 35 people were invited to the party.
 (i) The 'plane leaves at 5 o'clock in the morning.
 (j) 50 years ago the roads were not so dangerous as they are today.
10 Rewrite the following passages with the necessary punctuation.*
Begin a new line for each speaker:

 (a) i went to the information department to get information ideas about travelling south and if possible a job it seemed as if khartoum was going to be my home for some time and i was in no position to live like a tourist do you think i could get work i asked rather hesitantly for i was still thinking in terms of the u k where getting a job however humble takes a bit of organising i was yet to learn that in africa you get a job simply by opening your mouth and asking for one you type of course oh yes i think they need someone at the ministry of education i will find out said the p r o and he telephoned on the spot can you type stencils i had a vague recollection of once typing a stencil so i said i could

 (b) yes they do want a typist he announced putting the phone down you had better go along and see mr brooks are you sure you can type stencils i think so i said becoming alarmed theres nothing much to it is there oh yes there is he answered severely if you dont type evenly it will come out blotchy and be no good i began to have grave doubts about my ability to type stencils but a job would be water in the desert so i said even typing was what i was noted for and it sounded most interesting youd better take a taxi its a long way was the p r o s parting advice so i started walking

 (c) this was to be the first of my lessons on the general set up of working in africa i had started out on the trip without even knowing whether working in transit was allowed or if allowed whether it was possible in actual fact it is allowed and welcomed because in overseas territories there are always more jobs than people to fill them at home you might walk the streets looking for work in some parts of africa it is the employers who walk the streets looking for you and all on the level they honestly only want typists

* The passages in this exercise are taken from *Follow the Sun* by Jill Wordsworth (Robert Hale Ltd.).

(d) in sudan no office workers were recruited from home the positions were all filled by wives and families of officials who being independent switched jobs or gave up working altogether when they felt like it so there was always a vacancy going somewhere in the other territories trade is expanding faster than the population so even with some recruiting from overseas it is still a sellers market with salaries in certain parts such as the copper belt to make your eyes pop

(e) another mistake i had made was to assume that with plenty of strings to my bow i would be in a better position than with only one so i had collected experience in a vast number of occupations from highly technical ones down to selling cigarettes all this was quite unnecessary to work your way round the world you simply need to be able to type and nothing more this job has the advantage that employers are quite resigned to your leaving so that you can move on at any time without causing havoc and disruption

(f) typing was the one skill i had rather overlooked thinking that office work was an overcrowded profession and best avoided but in the wide open spaces even the offices are underpopulated and many a boss has to do his own letters and like it as a journalist i had to type but i never fancied myself as the perfect secretary and in fact privately considered perfect secretaries to be drips so that is how i came to be applying for a job typing stencils with only one stencil to my credit by way of recommendation

(g) mr brooks didnt take life too seriously and didnt seem unduly concerned about my ability these wretched stencils have all been done once he said but in this climate they dont keep so if we want more copies we have to make new stencils he explained that routine work was normally done by sudanese men confidential work by british women what i was to do was far from confidential but as it was an odd job it might as well be done by someone temporary but dont worry about running out of work he went on i can keep you busy for several months can you start tomorrow it was arranged that a car would call for me at the hotel each morning and that i should be paid a daily rate so as to be able to leave at once if a lift came along it was a wonderful arrangement

11 Write or type the following passage with correct punctuation.

John and I thought that you would like to hear some of our adventures when we went to europe last month it was quite a different kind of holiday from any other holiday which we had had in the past we were determined to do just as we wanted to as and when we wanted to without any planning or booking beforehand with this in mind we equipped ourselves with maps and guides especially those which gave all the eating places you know those delightful books with pictures of knives and forks and things they turned out to be most reliable we scarcely ever made a mistake in the choice of somewhere to eat but let me go back to the beginning and explain that we took the car and as we wanted to be in the sun as much as possible we were very extravagant and had a continental sun roof put on beforehand this didnt cost as much as we thought and was well worth it we both came back as brown as berries we wore shirts and shorts until we got really towards the south and after that I wore a sun top and shorts and John just wore shorts so that it wasnt just our faces that got the sun we were brown all over I know that you will envy us because I remember how you used to love just lying in the sun I have to confess at once that we did have to book the space for the car on the cross channel boat we dared not risk not getting on we got stuck once before in this manner and I was late for the beginning of term and there was dreadful trouble so we booked and got across very easily driving down to the coast the evening before we sailed and reaching france about midday it was pouring with rain as usual I dont think I have ever arrived in france when it wasnt raining but after we had been driving for about an hour the rain stopped and we were able to get along at quite a good pace and arrived at that charming place outside paris I never can remember the name you remember you and I and your sister had such a good meal there on our way back from the south we had dinner there and being lazy decided to stay the night in fact we stayed two days there exploring the countryside around which was so pretty the third day saw us on the way so we thought to the south of france but we lost our way and found ourselves in some vineyard country which was so interesting that we never got any further we found ourselves not only in beautiful country but staying with the most hospitable people a farmer his wife and two sons they took us right into their home and we had a real insight into the life of a farmer in this part of the country a hard life but very satisfactory and satisfying the car behaved very well and on the way back gave us no more trouble than one puncture I do wish that you and jim had been with us it would have been even more enjoyable please come and see us soon we have some beautiful slides to show you I will keep all the rest of the news until I see you how is your mother please give her my love

12 We are now giving you ten letters to retype. Some have no paragraphs and no punctuation. The earlier ones have been partly punctuated to help you understand.

The first two letters are already divided into paragraphs and have full stops in. We want you to put in the commas. The next two letters have the paragraphs (showing the division of thought) but no full stops. Here you must put in full stops and commas. After that you are on your own entirely. The letters get progressively difficult and the last two make use of most of the punctuating devices discussed in this chapter.

Letter 1
      (already has paragraphs and full stops—put in commas)

```
Dear John

       Thank you for your letter and invitation.  I think that
unexpected events excepted I can safely say I can be in town
next week.  If however anything happens to prevent me I shall
let you know immediately.
```

You do not say if you want me to come to your office or if you would prefer me on arrival to go straight to your home. When you send me particulars perhaps you will let me know this too.

Yours sincerely

Letter 2
(already has paragraphs and full stops—put in commas)

Dear Sir

Thank you for your letter in reply to my enquiry which was made in response to your advertisement in the Evening Standard.

I am interested to learn that the grand piano which you have for disposal is a Steinway and I shall be very glad to inspect this instrument. If convenient to you I should like to call at your house on Saturday next the 29th May arriving about 4 p.m. but if this time is not suitable perhaps you will kindly let me know.

As a matter of fact I really wish to exchange my small modern piano for a grand such as your Steinway and it occurs to me that you may be interested in such a proposition. This piano a Knight is in excellent condition in fact as new and has a beautiful tone. If you are interested perhaps we can discuss the matter when we meet.

Yours faithfully

Letter 3
(has paragraphs but no full stops—put in full stops and commas)

Dear Sir

I spoke to you on the telephone yesterday and you agreed to cut away some of the hawthorn trees growing in the next door garden but overhanging our drive since I spoke to you I have been unable to obtain the permission of all the occupants of the next door flats so that we must delay the operation until permission is obtained

At the same time perhaps you would be so good as to look in the back garden at the trees you lopped last year there seems to be a large dead branch on the oak at the bottom but I am not sure if you can reach it without ladders

Yours truly

Letter 4
(has paragraphs but not full stops—put in full stops and commas)

Dear Madam

Thank you for your letter of the 20th May asking us to reserve accommodation for you and your daughter from Friday 4th June to Sunday 27th June but we regret that for this period we have not available a double room with private bathroom

We could however offer you one single room with private bath and another single room on the same floor but on the opposite side of the corridor without bath alternatively we could offer you a double bedroom with shower this is a large room on the first floor and has a very pleasant outlook facing the sea

We look forward to receiving your instructions by return

Yours faithfully
for DOMINION HOTELS LIMITED

Letter 5
(has neither paragraphs nor punctuation—paragraph this, and punctuate with full stops and commas only)

Dear Sir we have received a letter from you asking us to send to you immediately your order for 10,000 cartons size M reference MS KS 210 we wish at once to inform you that the goods in question packed as you particularly requested in 100s were sent to you by British Rail ten days ago we are beginning an investigation from this end and should be extremely grateful if you would let us know immediately if you subsequently receive this first delivery in the meantime we are sending by special carrier a second consignment of cartons and hope that our action will help to ameliorate your difficult position in relation to the despatch of your goods urgently required for export yours faithfully

Letters 6–10
(should be paragraphed and punctuated by the use of all steps discussed. Capital letters should be used where necessary)

Letter 6

dear sirs reference membership no 2164a your application for legal assistance in dealing with a claim in connection with your recent accident has been passed to this department by the general secretary to whom you wrote it will be necessary for a member of this department not only to view your vehicle and the site of the accident but to have a fairly long discussion with you perhaps you would be good enough to telephone the writer of this letter to make such an appointment it would be helpful if the interview could take place at your home it would be helpful for us to have the answers to certain questions before the interview they are 1 are you the sole owner of the vehicle concerned 2 were you driving it on this occasion 3 if not who was the driver 4 what was the category of insurance under which the vehicle was insured we gather from your letter that you have already had considerable correspondence with your own insurance people on this topic they may care to be present at our meeting in view of the time that has already elapsed since the accident we should like to hear from you as soon as possible yours faithfully

Letter 7

messrs johnson & gillett 2 wigmore street w1 dear sirs on behalf of madame delfont I am replying to your letter of the 16th may before leaving for new york madame delfont instructed me to inform you that she will be pleased to accept the concert booking with the welsh philharmonic orchestra at st stephens hall cardiff on Friday 1st October 1975 the following are madame delfont's programme suggestions programme 1 piano concerto no 1 in c major beethoven scherzo in e flat minor brahms programme 2 piano concerto no 3 bartok impromptu in b flat major d 935 schubert i also enclose a selection of photographs and an up to date biography for inclusion in the programme on the question of the fee for this concert madame delfont will write to you herself as soon as she returns to london in about 10 days time she has however asked me to say that she is a little surprised to receive this request for a reduction in the fee of £250 as this figure was the one suggested by you when the concert was first discussed yours faithfully secretary to madame delfont

Letter 8

dear sir householders comprehensive insurance we have received a proposal form for the insurance of the contents of your house which we confirm is acceptable and are holding covered from 1st June 1975 the premium required is £15.75 and if you will be kind enough to let us have your remittance we shall be pleased to send you the necessary policy in reply to your enquiry this policy will not cover property more specifically insured or unless specially mentioned deeds bonds bills of exchange promissory notes cheques securities for money documents of any kind manuscripts medals and coins motor vehicles and accessories whilst thereon or live stock other than horses please also note that no one curio picture or other work of art stamp collection or article of gold silver or other precious metal jewellery or fur shall be deemed of greater value than five per cent of the full value of the contents as therein declared unless specially insured in a separate item and the total value of articles of gold silver or other precious metal jewellery or fur shall be deemed not to exceed one third of the full value of the contents unless specially agreed therein if there is any further information you require please telephone the undersigned yours truly

Letter 9

messrs smith smith & jones 12 old buildings lincolns inn wc2 dear sirs re fairhaven 26 park view stevenage herts thank you for your letter of yesterday's date from which I note that as a result of the advertisement in the daily telegraph mr and mrs e roberts are interested in the tenancy of the above property i return herwith the draft tenancy agreement which you were good enough to send me this appears to be satisfactory with the exception of the following 1 in clause 1 please alter for a term of 3 years to a term of 5 years in accordance with the decision made when we discussed the matter at your office last wednesday 2 do you consider it advisable to insert the following at the end of clause 7 subject to prior agreement being given in writing by the lessor the tenancy will of course be subject to three first class references being given by the proposed lessee i feel and i am sure you will agree that one of these should be from mr roberts employer i shall be glad to see a copy of the revised agreement at your early convenience and hope the matter can be concluded without delay as the house has been unoccupied for six months and i am anxious for the new tenants to move in before the autumn please communicate with my secretary if there are any points you wish to raise as i am just leaving for a 3 day trip to the north of england yours faithfully

Letter 10
(paragraph and punctuate, inserting capital letters, quotation marks and brackets)

```
the secretary animal supplies london ltd 4 pond street leighton yorks
dear sir ref show equipment white plastic thank you for your catalogue
from which we have selected certain items which we should be glad if
you would supply as soon as possible these items are listed below
bowls white plastic 7.5 cm diameter 2 doz bowls white plastic 12.5 cm
diameter 2 doz trays white plastic oblong 30 cm length ½ doz white
plastic oblong 40 cm length ½ doz white show blankets 90 cm by 30 cm
1 doz we note that you are able to print on the bowls and trays at
the owners request the name of the kennels we should be grateful to
know if the words low gates of ilstead could be printed in this
manner or is the title too long yours truly manager low gates kennels
```

EXERCISES

1 Write out the following passages with the correct punctuation, paying particular attention to inverted commas, apostrophes, and capital letters:

(i) my friend told me a riddle the other day whats the difference he asked between a gate and a moth flying round a candle i dont know i said well he told me as the gate goes on its hinges it swings and as the moth goes on it singes its wings.

(ii) the letter was addressed to a h jones esq bsc hope cottage mangle lane east ogsby lincs

(iii) the guest at the girls grammar school speech day on friday was lady gathercole the writer of up the amazon in a canvas canoe

2 Write sentences which illustrate the correct use of the following:
(*a*) apostrophe (')
(*b*) quotation marks (inverted commas) (' ')
(*c*) dash (—)
(*d*) question mark (?)
(*e*) hyphen (-)
You may use them in any order and may, if you wish, use more than one kind in any sentence.

3 Each of the following sentences can be punctuated in at least two different ways with, of course, a change of meaning. Write down each sentence, punctuated in *two* different ways.
For example: My father said John is a soldier.
    (*a*) 'My father,' said John, 'is a soldier.'
    (*b*) My father said, 'John is a soldier.'
 (i) What happened then I don't know.
 (ii) What did you write in your book John Smith.
 (iii) Where will you meet him in London.
 (iv) The teacher said the boy is a fool.

4 Write out the following passage with the necessary punctuation. Begin a new line for each speaker:

what a nice young lady miss emily is said mary the fat boy having finished his pie replied i know a nicer one indeed exclaimed mary yes indeed declared the fat boy whats her name asked mary whats yours said the fat boy mary she answered sos hers was the fat boys rejoinder.

5 Write out the following passage with the necessary punctuation. Begin a new line for each new speaker:

who are fighting again alice ventured to ask why the lion and the unicorn of course said the king fighting for the crown asked alice yes to be sure said the king and the best of the joke is that its my crown all the while lets run and see them he added

6 Punctuate and correctly arrange the following:

youd better let the local hotel people know when theyre coming mother remarked what for asked john surprised so that they can reserve the rooms said mother equally surprised but ive invited them to stay here here you havent really you are most thoughtless john they cant possibly stay now look here mother i really dont see what youre making all the fuss about but where are they going to sleep theres hardly enough room for us as it is nonsense theres plenty of room if nan and jim sleep on the veranda you and jack can sleep in the dont be silly dear we cant camp all over the place youll just have to write and put these people off i cant theyre on their way

7 Write the following passage, correctly set out and punctuated. In the passage as printed there are five spelling errors. Correct the five words and underline each one:

Lawyers hold that there are two kinds of particularly bad witnesses a reluctant witness and à to willing witnesss it was Mr Winkles fate to figure in both characters I will even go further than this Mr Winkle continued Mr Phunky in a most smooth and complasent manner did you ever see anything in Mr Pickwicks manner and conduct towards the opposite sex to induce you to believe that he ever contemplated matrimony of late years in any case oh no certainly not has his behaviour when females have been in the case always been that of a man who having attained a pretty advanced period of life content with his own occupations and amusments treats them only as a father might his daughters not the least doubt of it replied Mr Winkle in the fulness of his heart that is yes oh yes certainly you have never known anything in his behaviour towards Mrs Bardell or any other female in the least degree suspicious n n no replied Mr Winkle except on one trifling occasion which I have no doubt might be easily explained

8 Punctuate each of the following sentences in two different ways. Underneath each of your four answers explain how the punctuation affects the meaning of the answer:

   (a) What do you think this man made fibre will sell for as much as the best silk
   (b) Many shopkeepers I know no longer sell these goods

9 Write the following with correct punctuation:

now george says mr bucket duty is duty and friendship is friendship i never want the two to clash if i can help it you must consider yourself in custody george custody what for returns the trooper thunderstruck now george says mr bucket duty as you very well know is one thing and conversation is another its my duty to inform you that any observations you may make will be liable to be used against you therefore george be careful what you say you dont happen to have heard of a murder murder now george says mr bucket bear in mind what ive said to you i ask you nothing youve been in low spirits this afternoon i say you dont happen to have heard of a murder no where has there been a murder now george says mr bucket im agoing to tell you theres been a murder in lincolns inn fields gentleman by the name of tulkinghorn he was shot last night i want you for that

10 Punctuate the following:

The proprietor of the cafe saw them coming when they were still a long way off the lamps at that time were still alight it was later that the bullets broke the bulbs and dropped darkness all over that quarter of paris and the group showed up plainly in the wide barren boulevard since sunset only one customer had entered the café.

11 Type the following sentences, inserting the necessary punctuation.

   (a) Why is it that in spite of our ever increasing expenditure on education so many people in this country are incapable of expressing themselves clearly demanded councillor jones
   (b) Write to mrs robinson said the director to his secretary to ask her if she can recommend a really first class ladies and gentlemens outfitter

12 Type the following passage, punctuating it correctly.

possibly the biggest single difference between british and american eating habits lies in the latter's acceptance of minced meat hamburger vienna steak and meat loaf are the chief features of their menu we prefer to be able to identify our meat salad a top favourite with americans is far more interesting than in this country they insist that it be colourful fresh ice cold and beautifully arranged sandwiches also vary considerably we have a filling between two slices of bread or roll but they call a ten oz steak on a postage stamp of bread a sandwich

Spelling

I take it you already know
Of tough and bough and cough and dough?
Others may stumble, but not you
On hiccough, thorough, lough, and through?
Well done! And now you wish, perhaps,
To learn of less familiar traps?

Beware of heard, a dreadful word
That looks like beard and sounds like bird,
And dead: it's said like bed, not bead—
For goodness sake don't call it 'deed'!
Watch out for meat and great and threat
(They rhyme with suite and straight and debt).

A moth is not a moth in mother
Nor both in bother, broth in brother,
And here is not a match for there
Nor dear and fear for bear and pear,
And then there's dose and rose and lose—
Just look them up—and goose and choose,

And cork and work and card and ward,
And font and front and word and sword,
And do and go and thwart and cart—
Come, come, I've hardly made a start!
A dreadful language? Man alive,
I'd mastered it when I was five.

Let us begin by agreeing with the author of this poem that English spelling is very difficult. There are few rules; there are many exceptions; some people have great difficulty in remembering how to spell even the simplest and commonest words, whilst others never make a spelling mistake.

Are these people who never make spelling mistakes exceptionally clever? No, good spelling has nothing to do with cleverness; some of the most brilliant men and women are not, by nature, good spellers. How then do they avoid making spelling mistakes? The answer is that they are aware of the words they *cannot* spell and before writing these words they look them up in a dictionary.

This may be called the secret of correct spelling: take the trouble to look up in a dictionary words about which you are uncertain. Don't be lazy and don't be optimistic about your spelling; be aware of the words which cause you trouble; always look them up in a dictionary before using them and you will find that the number of words you need to look up gradually decreases.

Spelling rules

Here are a few spelling rules. Read them through and try to understand and apply them. You may find that the arrangement of the words in lists under sub-headings will help you to think more clearly about groups of words which you have previously found confusing.

Some people find the rules are so complicated and the exceptions so numerous that it is easier for them to learn the words individually. Indeed recent research shows that in some cases spelling lists are more useful than spelling rules. If, when you have read through the rules, you think you will improve your spelling more quickly and more easily by learning from a spelling list, you will find some suggestions to help you on pages 40–42.

Whether you use spelling rules or spelling lists is immaterial. The most important consideration is to ensure that you never make a spelling mistake in anything you write or type. The most irritating error in transcription is the spelling error, and if you do not know how words *should* be spelt you will never be able to recognise and correct errors in your transcripts before presenting them for signature.

Hoping/Hopeing

1 Words ending in consonant-e . . .

	(a) *drop the 'e' before a vowel suffix*		(b) *remain unchanged before a consonant suffix*
hope	hoped hoping	hope	hopeful hopeless

change	changed changing	change	changeless
wire	wired wiring	wire	wireless
excite	excited exciting excitable	excite	excitement
manage	managed managing	manage	management
move	moved moving movable	move	movement

Note: changeable, manageable, noticeable

Wrapped/Wraped?

2 Single syllable words having a short vowel and ending in a single consonant . . .

	(a) *double the consonant before a vowel suffix*	(b) *remain unchanged before a consonant suffix*	
hop	hopped hopping		
shop	shopped shopping	shop	shopful
wrap	wrapper wrapping wrapped		
ship	shipped shipping	ship	shipment shipyard
win	winning winner		

Occurred/Occured?

3 Polysyllabic words, ending in vowel-r, vowel-t, or vowel-n . . .

	(a) *and when accented on the last syllable, double the final consonant before all suffixes*	(b) *remain unchanged before all suffixes when the first syllable of the word is accented*
occur	occurred occurring occurrence	

prefer	preferred	prefer	preferable
	preferring		preference
begin	beginning		
	beginner		
allot	allotted	benefit	benefited
	allotting		benefiting

Note: inhabit—inhabited, inhabiting, inhabitant, allotment, preferment, deferment

Traveler/Traveller?

4 Polysyllabic words ending in l . . .

(a) double the 'l' before a vowel suffix		(b) remain unchanged before a consonant suffix	
enrol	enrolled	enrol	enrolment
	enrolling		
revel	revelled	revel	revelry
	reveller		
annul	annulled	annul	annulment
travel	traveller		
	travelled		
	travelling		
install	installed	install	instalment

Note: unparalleled, revelation, travelogue

Applied/Applyed?

5 Words ending in consonant-y . . .

(a) change the 'y' to 'i' before -ed, -er and -es		(b) remain unchanged before -ing, -ist and consonant suffixes	
copy	copied	copy	copying
	copies		copyist
	copier		copyholder
			copyright
dry	dries	dry	drying
	dried		
	drier		
sky	skies	sky	skyline
	skied		skyscraper

apply	applied	apply	applying
	applies		
pity	pitied	pity	pitying
	pities		

Note: pitiful, pitiless, piteous

Wierd/Weird?

6 *ie* and *ei* words: i comes before e (believe, relieve)

(a)	(b)
except after 'c'	*or when rhyming with ay*
receive	weigh
deceive	sleigh
receipt	neighbour
perceive	beige
ceiling	reign (sovereign, foreign)
	skein
	rein

Note: forfeit, seize, counterfeit, either, neither, height, weird, leisure

ible or able?...   *...ANT or ENT?*

Trigger words

This section deals with what we shall call 'trigger' words, by which we mean words which frequently cause trouble; whenever you are about to write, type or transcribe one of these words, an imaginary signal should trigger off in your head to warn you to consult a dictionary unless you are completely sure that you know the right spelling. Approach these words with caution; if you have learnt Latin or Greek (and can remember your declensions) you may know the explanation for the choices between *ible* and *able* and *ance* and *ence*; but for the majority of us they will remain 'trigger' words until we have finally committed them to memory.

ible or able?

able

acceptable	adaptable	advisable	agreeable
applicable	amicable	affable	amenable
available	comparable	capable	changeable
chargeable	controllable	despicable	dependable
detestable	debatable	desirable	durable
excitable	excusable	enviable	equitable
formidable	hospitable	inflammable	inevitable
imaginable	implacable	irritable	irrevocable
justifiable	lamentable	likeable	malleable
manageable	memorable	notable	probable
portable	preferable	profitable	pliable
practicable	questionable	reliable	taxable
tolerable	undeniable	venerable	vulnerable

ible

audible	accessible	admissible	credible
corruptible	crucible	contemptible	convertible
destructible	defensible	divisible	discernible
digestible	edible	fallible	feasible
flexible	gullible	horrible	incomprehensible
incredible	impossible	indelible	intelligible
invisible	irresistible	legible	negligible
plausible	possible	responsible	sensible
terrible	tangible	visible	reversible

ance or ence?

ance

abeyance	abundance	accordance	acquaintance
assurance	attendance	clearance	compliance
fragrance	grievance	guidance	relevance
reluctance	reliance	resistance	admittance
contrivance	ignorance	remittance	allowance

37

ambulance	appearance	assistance	conveyance
distance	entrance	endurance	extravagance
insurance	importance	maintenance	nuisance
performance	perseverance	substance	tolerance
vengeance	temperance	sustenance	defiance

ence

absence	adherence	affluence	audience
benevolence	commence	competence	conference
confidence	consequence	convenience	deference
eloquence	excellence	existence	experience
impatience	impertinence	incompetence	inference

influence	innocence	insistence	intelligence
negligence	obedience	occurrence	persistence
preference	presence	prominence	recurrence
reference	residence	reticence	sentence
subsistence	consistence	quintessence	obsolescence

ant or ent?

ant

1	2	3	4
abundant	accountant	applicant	assistant
attendant	descendant	distant	dominant
elegant	important	inhabitant	irrelevant
insignificant	lieutenant	observant	reluctant
remnant	resistant	resonant	restaurant

ent

1	2	3	4
abhorrent	absent	adjacent	affluent
ancient	benevolent	client	competent
component	concurrent	constituent	convalescent
convenient	correspondent	current	delinquent
different	diligent	efficient	eloquent

5	6	7	8
eminent	evident	excellent	expedient
exponent	frequent	imminent	impatient
incoherent	incompetent	inconsistent	innocent
insolent	intelligent	magnificent	permanent
persistent	prominent	resident	superintendent

dependant/ent. The noun has -*ant,* rarely -*ent;* the adjective -*ent,* rarely -*ant*.

er or or?

er

1	2	3	4
advertiser	adviser	beginner	character
consumer	designer	employer	eraser
foreigner	lawyer	manager	manufacturer
passenger	shipper	subscriber	treasurer

or

1	2	3	4
accelerator	actor	administrator	auditor
author	aviator	bachelor	commentator
competitor	conductor	contractor	creditor
debtor	dictator	distributor	doctor
duplicator	editor	escalator	governor

5	6	7	8
indicator	inferior	inventor	investigator
operator	proprietor	radiator	refrigerator
solicitor	spectator	sponsor	successor
superior	supervisor	surveyor	survivor
tabulator	tailor	tractor	traitor

sede, cede or ceed?

sede (only one word)	*ceed (only three words)*	*cede (all the rest)*
supersede	succeed	accede
	proceed	secede
	exceed	intercede
		procede
		concede
		recede

ise or ize?

(a)	(b)	(c)	
must have ise	*must have ize*	*either correct but the O.E.D. prefers*	
			ize
advertise	sympathize	criticise	criticize
exercise	pulverize	organise	organize
supervise		italicise	italicize
devise		apologise	apologize
revise		realise	realize
advise		recognise	recognize
excise		standardise	standardize
franchise		specialise	specialize
merchandise			
improvise			

cial or tial?

beneficial	deferential
artificial	preferential
social	essential
official	residential
	initial
	partial
	martial

'Please yourself' words*

These words may be spelt in two ways. If you consult Fowler's *Modern English Usage* you will find that some spellings are preferred to others. If you are still training, the most important thing is for you to be consistent in your choice of spelling; when you are at work, you must follow the preference expressed by your executive.

acknowledgment	acknowledgement
abridgment	abridgement
judgment	judgement
dispatch	despatch
inquire	enquire
by-law	bye-law
grey	gray
show	shew
net	nett

We started this chapter by saying that the secret of good spelling is to learn the words you cannot spell. The aim of every audio-typist, shorthand-typist and secretary must be to minimise the number of words

* If you would like to know why these words may be spelt in two ways read Chapter 8 of *Spelling* by G. H. Vallins (Andre Deutsch, 1965).

she needs to look up in the dictionary so that her work output is not slowed down by too many pauses to refer to the dictionary.

If you have learnt the spelling rules and become aware of the 'trigger' words you will be well on your way to becoming a good speller. What more can you do? Here are some suggestions.

1 Be enthusiastic about spelling. Read as widely and as much as possible and write down any new words you come across in a notebook.

2 Take a pride in becoming known as a 'good speller'. Eschew spelling mistakes as carefully as you should eschew chipped nail varnish or laddered tights. (And if you don't know the word 'eschew', why not start your spelling book now?)

3 Devise mnemonics for words that cause you particular difficulty. (A mnemonic is a memory aid.) Here are some mnemonics which you may find helpful:

> There's A RAT in sepARATe,
> 'lose' or 'loose'? 'Lose' has lost an 'o'.
> A stationer sells paper—hence stationery

4 Learn five words each day from the following list of words most frequently misspelt. Read the words carefully, write them many times, say to yourself and use them, until you know them as well as you know your own name.

Spelling list

1	2	3	4
abscess	accede	accelerate	accessible
accessory	accommodate	accumulate	achieve
acquaintance	acquiesce	acquitted	adjustable
admissible	adolescent	advantageous	advisability
aerial	aeroplane	agreeable	argument

5	6	7	8
allotted	absent	annihilate	anonymous
antecedent	appalling	auxiliary	assassinate
beginning	autumn	beneficial	benefited
believe	business	calendar	changeable
chaos	chargeable	circuit	commemorate

9	10	11	12
committee	comparatively	compatible	concession
concurrence	connoisseur	conscientious	conscious
consistency	correspondence	corroborate	definite
deferred	deficiency	descendant	develop
development	disappear	disappoint	discernible

13	14	15	16
discreet	dissatisfied	dissimilar	eccentric
efficacious	eligible	embarrass	emigrant
enrolment	esteem	exaggerate	exigency
existence	exorbitant	experience	extravagant
fascinate	favourite	forestall	fulfil

17	18	19	20
fulfilled	fulfilment	gauge	government
grievance	guarantee	harass	honorary
humorist	humorous	identical	illegible
immigrant	imminent	immovable	incoherent
incorrigible	indefensible	indictment	ineligible

21	22	23	24
inexhaustible	inflammable	innocuous	insistence
install	instalment	irrelevant	irresistible
itinerary	leisure	livelihood	manageable
manoeuvre	Mediterranean	meteorological	miniature
miscellaneous	mischievous	misdemeanour	movable

25	26	27	28
murmur	necessary	negligible	neighbour
noticeable	nuisance	occasionally	occurred
occurrence	paraffin	parallel	paralleled
Parliament	pavilion	perforate	permissible
pneumatic	poignant	possession	precede

29	30	31	32
preferred	prejudice	privilege	proceed
procedure	profession	proffered	promissory
psychological	quarrelled	queue	recede
receipt	receive	recommend	recompense
reference	referred	regrettable	relevant

33	34	35	36
relieve	reminiscent	remodelled	reprieve
resistance	resistible	reticent	retrieve
rhyme	rhythm	secede	sedentary
seize	separate	sergeant	serviceable

37	38	39	40
siege	simultaneous	sincerely	singeing
skilful	subterranean	succeed	successful
superintendent	supersede	survivor	technical
transferred	undoubtedly	unnecessary	unparalleled
vaccinate	vacillate	weird	woollen

EXERCISES

1 Write or type the following words inserting *ei* or *ie* as required:

    v--l   f--nt
    rec--ve   w--gh
    bel--f   for--gn
    s--ze   s--ge
    sover--gn   w--rd
    fr--ze   b--ge
    l--sure   r--ndeer
    p--rce   f--nd
    n--ce   s--ve
    f--gn   l--u

Consult the dictionary to check your answers. Write any new word in your vocabulary book, and alongside each word write its meaning.

2 Write or type the following words adding the correct suffix *ible* or *able*:

    toler-ble   irrepar-ble
    feas-ble   incorrig-ble
    sens-ble   incomprehens-ble
    enjoy-ble   manage-ble
    indefens-ble   ris-ble
    inexor-ble   convert-ble
    suit-ble   agree-ble

Consult the dictionary to check your answers. Write any new word in your vocabulary book, and alongside each word write its meaning.

3 Write or type the following words adding the correct suffix, *ance* or *ence*:

    dist-nce   intellig-nce
    temper-nce   sent-nce
    excell-nce   mainten-nce
    exist-nce   relev-nce
    nuis-nce   neglig-nce

Consult the dictionary to check your answers. Write any new word in your vocabulary book, and alongside each word write its meaning.

4 Complete the following words:

    autu-n   poi-ant
    accum-late   super-ede
    hon-rary   min-ature
    hum-rous   itin-rary
    inel-gible   a-roplane

Consult the dictionary to check your answers. Write any new word in your vocabulary book, and alongside each word write its meaning.

5 Complete the following words by inserting the correct single or double letters:

    sho(p)ing   para(f)in
    begi(n)er   unpara(l)eled
    benefi(t)ed   wra(p)er
    insta(l)ed   po(s)e(s)ion
    enro(l)ment   quinte(s)ence
    i(r)itable   i(m)igrant
    contro(l)able   su(c)e(s)or
    occu(r)ence   co(m)i(t)ee
    a(c)uracy   co(m)emorate
    ma(l)eable   ne(c)e(s)ary

Consult the dictionary to check your answers. Write any new word in your vocabulary book, and alongside each word write its meaning.

6 Write or type the following words and underline any letters that are not pronounced:

    pneumatic   salmon
    honest   knight
    hotel   psychological
    gnat   Gloucester
    psalm   viscount

7 You are chosen to represent your school in a Spelling Bee being 'organised by a local schools' organisation. Describe some steps you could take to prepare yourself for this event.

8 Your twelve year old sister finds great difficulty in learning how to spell correctly. Your parents ask you to help her. What advice would you give?

9 Your employer hands you a letter you had presented for signature and says 'You'll have to type this again. Why can't you learn how to spell?' The words he has ringed are: *acknowledgement, by-law, show, inquiry, recognise*. What would you say and do?

10 All the following words contain spelling errors. Write the words correctly.

    proceedure   immediately
    instalation   prominant
    referrence   accumalator
    batchelor   inhabitted
    speaches   disaggreable

11 This passage contains errors of Spelling, Punctuation and Grammar. Rewrite it, correcting where necessary.

Walking down the lane in search of accomodation, a little thatched cottage came into view, it had a sign which read, bed and breakfast. 'Its just what we want, cried Mother. Arrangements were soon completed for us to stay for a week. Everyone felt that their wishes had come true—A whole week in a cottage by the sea!

12 Some adjectives are formed by adding the suffix 'able' or 'ible' to the original words. Sometimes the letter 'e' is omitted, e.g. 'excite' becomes 'excitable'. Make an adjective from each of the following words:

>contempt
>response
>access
>contest
>move

A CHOIR OF PAPER?
A QUIRE OF PAPER?...

3

Homophones

Homophones* are words which have the same sound but different spelling and different meaning or function. Owing to the vagaries of spelling and the varied derivation of the English language, it contains many pairs or groups of homophones, e.g. *pair, pare, pear; cue, queue, Kew; mayor, mare.*

Homophones are stock-in-trade words for the comedian and scriptwriter. As you are listening to stage, radio or television comedians you will notice that many of the jokes are built around homophones, such as the old story about the boy in class who said, 'Sorry, Sir, I'm a little hoarse today', and the teacher replied, 'That's funny, you were a little monkey yesterday.'

For the transcriber, however, homophones present serious problems. Homophones are another set of 'trigger' words, that is (as we discussed in Chapter 2, Spelling) words which must be treated with great caution. Whenever you see the shorthand outline for a homophone, or hear a homophone (if you are typing from recorded dictation), you must pause and consider which spelling is required within the context of the sentence you are typing.

Most homophones must be learnt by rote. In some cases you may find you can make a mnemonic which will help you, such as—

'Principle' or 'principal'? A *pal* is a person, so 'princi*pal*' is the spelling for the person who is head of a school or college.

'Their' or 'there'? *'Here'* indicates place, so *'there'* also indicates place.

All the commonest homophones are listed in this chapter. You should aim eventually to know them by heart. In the meantime you will be well on the way to mastering them if you make yourself aware of all the out-

---

* Homonyms are words which are identical in form (i.e. spelling), but of different meanings. E.g. **sage** which means either **a herb** or **a wise man**.

lines or spoken words which can be spelt in more than one way, and take the trouble to refer to the lists and consider the context before typing. For example, whenever you see the outline for 'practice/se', you must ask yourself 'Is the word a noun or a verb in this sentence?' Some people say to themselves, 'I can *see* (c) a noun, therefore 'c' for the noun 'practice', 's' for the verb.'

So that you can refer easily to the lists, each pair or group of words has been arranged alphabetically (*allowed* precedes *aloud*), and the groups or pairs have been indexed according to the first word of the group or pair (*all, awl,* precede *allowed, aloud*).

When one of the words commences with a different letter of the alphabet, the group or pair has also been indexed in the second alphabetical group, e.g. *cue, Kew* and *queue* appear in the 'C'. 'K' and 'Q' sections; *ceiling* and *sealing* appear in both the 'C' and 'S' sections. There is a dotted line beside each word, on which you can write the shorthand outline for the word.

aid or aide?

aid	....	(n) help, assistance; (v) to help, to assist With the aid of the librarian, the girl found the book. White sticks aid the blind.
aide	....	a personal assistant The secretary was appointed aide to the manager.
air	....	the atmosphere surrounding the earth All rooms should have a supply of fresh air.
heir	....	next in line to property or position when the present holder dies or retires He is heir to his father's lands.
aisle	....	passages between seats in a church or place of public entertainment The usherette showed them to their seats next to the aisle.
isle	....	a small area of land surrounded by water (often poetic) 'This sceptered isle . . . England, bound in with the triumphant sea.'
I'll	....	contraction of *I shall* or *I will* (emphatic future) I'll go now. I'll go, in spite of what you say.
all	....	everyone, everything All sing together. All the trunks are packed.
awl	....	carpenter's tool for pricking He used the awl to mark the screw-holes.

allowed	....	permitted They were allowed an hour for lunch. He allowed his wife £10 for housekeeping.
aloud	....	speaking, not in a whisper She read the letter aloud to the meeting.
alms	....	gifts of money or kind to charity The Queen distributes Maundy Alms.
arms	....	the upper limbs of the body of a primate She carried the baby in her arms.
all ready	....	everything, everyone prepared Is all ready for the party? We are all ready.
already	....	beforehand, previously I have already answered this letter. The room was already prepared for the meeting.
altar	....	Communion Table: central place of sacrifice to the gods The priest stood at the altar for the service
alter	....	to change Because of fog, the railways had to alter the times of the trains.
all together	....	collected in a group The letters were all together in the file.
altogether	....	completely, on the whole The work was altogether different from my last post.
analyst	....	a person skilled in breaking down compounds into their elements The analyst told the meeting which gases combine to make air.
annalist	....	a recorder of events, year by year The annalist kept a daily record of events for many years.
arc	....	part of the circumference of a circle A rainbow makes an arc in the sky.
ark	....	a box; Noah's ship at the time of the Deluge The Ark of the Covenant stands in the Synagogue.
ascent	....	upward movement or way up The ascent of Everest was a fine achievement. The ascent of the stairs left her breathless.
assent	....	expression of agreement He gave his assent to the proposals.

assistance	....	the giving of aid
		Without her assistance, we should not have finished the task.
assistants	....	helpers
		The assistants were thanked by the manager for their help in the sales rush.
attendance	....	group of people present at a meeting etc.
		There was a good attendance at the shareholders' meeting.
attendants	....	servants
		The attendants handed round the copies of the papers.
aught	....	anything
		For aught one knows, he may still be standing on the station.
ought	....	expresses duty or probability
		We ought to have answered this letter before. The favourite ought to win the race.
auger	....	a tool with a screw point used for boring
		The engineer used an auger for drilling the well.
augur	....	to give a prophecy
		The year's trading figures augur well for the future.

bail or bale?

bail	....	(n) security for release; (v) to release on security
		The prisoner was granted bail on security of £100.
bail/bale	....	(v) to remove water from a flooded area with a bucket etc.
		The crew had to bail the boat out during the storm.
bale	....	compressed bundle of material, e.g. cloth, hay.
		The retailer unwrapped a bale of cotton.
ball	....	spherical object used in games
		The children broke the window with a football.
bawl	....	to shout out
		The man bawled across the room for his newspaper.
base	....	the bottom, the foundations, mean
		The statue stood on a marble base. The base actions of the villain were the cause of the trouble.
bass	....	deepest sounding
		He sang bass in the choir.

baron	....	a member of the lowest order of nobility
		The Baron sat in the House of Lords.
barren	....	unable to bear life; profitless
		The desert is a barren tract of land. The members were barren of ideas on how to raise money for the club.
beach	....	(n) stretch of sand; (v) to pull a boat onto dry land
		Children build castles on the beach. The boat was beached for the winter.
beech	....	a deciduous tree
		The leaves of the beech turn golden-red in the autumn.
bear	....	(n) a large quadruped; (v) to carry, to speculate for a fall in stocks etc.
		The broker created a bear by selling the stock.
bare	....	nude, without disguise
		Bare arms are cold in winter. He listed the bare facts.
beat	....	to whip; to defeat
		Beat the eggs well. The champion beat all comers.
beet	....	an agricultural plant
		Beet is a valuable source of sugar.
berry	....	the fruit of certain plants, trees and shrubs
		Many plants bear colourful berries in the winter.
bury	....	to place underground; to be absorbed in; to cover up
		He was buried in his father's grave. She was buried in a book. The papers were buried on his desk.
berth	....	room for a ship to swing at anchor or tie up; sleeping-place; appointment
		She docked at berth 19 this morning. Book me a berth to Holland on Friday. Her new post seems a good berth.
birth	....	act of being born
		The birth of the baby was announced in the papers.
board	....	long piece of timber; provision of meals to a lodger; government department
		We must have a new floor-board. The charge for full board is £8 a day. The Local Government Board must be consulted.
bored	....	made tired by tiresome talk etc.; dug a small hole for water, etc.
		The gossiper bored everyone with her tales. They bored two hundred feet down to find water.

boarder	....	a paying guest who receives food as well as lodging
		Many seaside landladies take boarders in the summer.
border	....	edge of a country; piece of land, material etc.
		He crossed the border between England and Scotland.
bold	....	brave
		The bold soldier was given a medal.
bowled	....	delivered a ball
		He once bowled for England.
bolder	....	braver, more impudent
		The bolder of the two boys spoke up first.
boulder	....	a large lump of rock
		The boulder had to be moved to reach the mouth of the cave.
born	....	come into the world by birth
		He was born on Midsummer's Day.
borne	....	endured
		Toothache has to be borne (with) until one has seen the dentist. His bad temper is not to be borne (with).
borough	....	a town which has been granted privileges by royal charter
		It is the duty of a borough to provide many social services within the town.
burrow	....	to dig deeply into something
		I must burrow in my desk to find the papers.
boy	....	young male human
		The ten year old boy asked for a space-ship for his birthday.
buoy	....	(n) an anchored float used as a navigational aid; (v) to sustain
		The buoy marked the channel into the harbour. The men in the lifeboat buoyed up their spirits with singing.
brake	....	(v) to stop; (n) device for stopping vehicles
		The driver had to brake suddenly. Please test the brakes on my car.
break	....	to divide into two or more parts but not by cutting; to weaken
		Pottery will break if you drop it. The new disasters will break his spirit.

breach	....	(v) to break a gap in something; (n) a breaking or neglect of duties
		The attacks breach the defences of the town. Failure to deliver the goods will be a breach of the contract.
breech	....	the back part of a gun barrel; (pl.) a pair of breeches, short trousers
		Breech-loading guns improved the speed of reloading.
bread	....	flour mixture raised with leaven
		Bread is sold in loaves of many shapes.
bred	....	raised
		She bred black spaniels.
bridal	....	belonging to a bride
		The bridal bouquet was made of white carnations.
bridle	....	the part of the harness that is worn on the head
		Good riders need only the bridle to control the horse.
broach	....	to begin a discussion; to open a cask, cargo, etc.
		The subject was broached at the last meeting and we shall discuss it fully later. He broached the keg of ale.
brooch	....	an ornamental safety-pin
		She wore a brooch of pearls on her lapel.
but	....	except, only
		They are all wrong but him. He is but a child yet.
butt	....	(n) target for shooting; (v) hit with the head
		Archers practise at the butts. The goats butt people in defence.
buy	....	purchase
		We must buy some new furniture.
by	....	along; before
		We will go by the nearest road. It will be finished by tonight.
bye	....	subordinate (often a prefix);
		The Borough Council passed a new bye-law about the use of the parks.

calendar or calender

calendar	....	table of dates for a given year; register chronologically arranged The calendar will tell you on what day of the week 1st July falls this year.
calender	....	a steam press for finishing laundry, paper etc. Sheets are put through the calender after washing and before they are returned by the laundry.
cannon	....	a mounted gun A cannon must be mounted firmly before firing.
canon	....	Church law, member of the cathedral chapter The canon discussed the new canon issued by the Archbishop.
canvas	....	specially prepared material for painting, tents etc. The canvas of the tent was laid out to dry.
canvass	....	find out views, ideas etc. A canvass of the area disclosed that most people wanted new street-lighting.
carat	....	the measure of weight for precious stones and gold The two carat diamond was set in twenty-two carat gold.
caret	....	a mark put below the line to show omission A caret was put to indicate that the 'h' had been missed out.
carrot	....	an orange-coloured root vegetable Carrots are served in the winter.
cast	....	to throw; to shape The javelin was cast into the air. The statue was cast in bronze.
caste	....	class divisions in India Members in one caste do not have any social contacts with people not of their caste.
caught	....	past tense of 'to catch' He caught the train last night.
court	....	area surrounded by high walls, residence of a sovereign, assembly of judges, magistrates etc. He walked through the gates into the lower court of the castle. The driver is giving evidence in court today.

cede	....	yield
		Gibraltar was ceded by Spain to Britain many years ago.
seed	....	the part of the fruit of a plant that grows into a new plant
		He spent Sunday afternoon sewing gardenia seeds.
ceiling	....	the top of a room; the top price, wages; highest level of flight etc.
		The new plane flies at a ceiling of 75,000 feet.
sealing	....	securing with wax etc.; placing a seal on a document, in addition to a signature, to show that the document is genuine
		The sealing of the contract took place in front of four witnesses.
cell	....	small room in a monastery or prison; smallest living unit
		The amoeba is a single-cell animal.
sell	....	to find purchasers for goods, property etc.
		Co-operatives sell many kinds of merchandise.
cellar	....	space under a building often used for storage
		Coal used to be shot into the cellar.
seller	....	one who sells
		The seller made a profit of a pound on the deal.
censer	....	incense burner
		Catholic churches have censers for the incense.
censor	....	one who controls the issuing of plays, books, news, etc. on grounds of morals, sedition or national expediency
		Films shown in England are classified by the censor.
cent	....	division of a hundred
		A cent is one hundredth part of a dollar. Interest is quoted at so much per cent.
scent	....	a pleasant smell; the smell of an animal
		Women love French scent. The hounds follow the scent of the fox.
sent	....	past tense of 'to send'
		The goods were sent yesterday.
cereal	....	grain crops
		The cereal crops of North America are wheat and maize.
serial	....	part of a series; narrative published in instalments
		Many magazines publish serial stories which run for several issues.

cession	....	surrendering rights in property or land The cession of Hong Kong to Britain gave the British a port in China.
session	....	uninterrupted period of time for the discussion of business The board was in session for five hours on Monday to discuss the new factory.
cheap	....	not expensive; poor in quality Fruit is cheap this week. The dress looked cheap.
cheep	....	noise made by a bird, especially the young birds Hungry nestlings cheep loudly for food.
check	....	to stop; to go over something to ensure accuracy Please check the typists who leave early. The figures need to be checked again.
cheque	....	written order to a banker to pay money to someone Payments may be made by cash or cheque; in the latter case receipts are not normally issued.
choir	....	a group of singers Vocal works performed at the Promenade concerts often require a large choir.
quire	....	24 sheets of writing paper; any number of bound leaves in a book Poor typists need a quire of paper for one letter.
chord	....	harmonising group of notes played at the same time He struck a chord on the piano.
cord	....	rope of various thicknesses The man tied a cord round the bundle to secure it.
cite	....	to quote Lawyers often cite precedents in court.
sight	....	ability to see; a spectacle; an invention to help in aiming or observing Engine drivers must have good sight. The Lord Mayor's Show is a sight to remember. Turn your sights on to that ship to identify her.
site	....	ground on which a building or town stood, stands or is to stand The new factory site is just outside Glasgow.

chews	....	grinds with the teeth; thinks over The dog chews a bone. The inventor chews over the idea for a long time.
choose	....	select, pick out You can choose any chocolate you like.
coarse	....	rough, vulgar Crash is a coarse linen material. Coarse jokes often cause embarrassed laughter.
course	....	route; division of a meal; line of bricks etc.; track for racing The ship continued on its course. Soup was served as the first course. The wall was twelve courses high. Derby Sunday brings many people to look at the course.
collar	....	a neckband; band or ring in machinery Puritans wore large white collars. The two pipes were joined by a collar of brass.
choler	....	anger, bad-temper Choler turned his face red.
confidant	....	one entrusted with another's secrets The confidant knew all her mistress's secrets.
confident	....	sure of something He was confident that he could meet the order before the date required.
compare	....	to look for likenesses between two things They compared the two photographs.
compére	....	the arranger of a cabaret who introduces the artistes and may comment on the different acts The compère told us that the next act was a singer.
complacent	....	smug There was a complacent grin on his face when his horse won.
complaisant	....	showing a desire to act according to someone's wishes The complaisant shop-keeper was very popular with the customers.

complement	....	that which completes
		The ship carries a complement of 600 men. The couple were the perfect complement to each other.
compliment	....	a pleasant comment, not necessarily true
		Her employer paid her the compliment of saying that her letters always looked so nice.
core	....	centre, heart
		He threw away the apple core. The narrow pipe, making the core of the well, was sunk yesterday.
corps	....	unit of soldiers who perform special duties
		The Intelligence Corps gained much information from the enemy.
correspondence	....	agreement, letters
		The correspondence between the answers of the witnesses proved the case. The correspondence columns of *The Times* often have amusing letters.
correspondents	....	letter-writers, journalists who write special types of news for their papers
		I collect foreign stamps because our firm has correspondents in many countries. *The Times* correspondent in India accompanied Sir John Hunt's expedition to Everest.
council	....	a group of people assembled to give advice or discuss matters
		The British Council is responsible for giving cultural information abroad about Britain.
counsel	....	(n) advice; (v) advise
		The Citizens' Advice Bureau gives counsel on many points. I counsel you to see a solicitor about the problem.
councillor	....	member of a council
		He has been elected councillor for the ward.
counsellor	....	one who gives advice
		Marriage guidance counsellors work in many areas.
crews	....	bodies of men who operate a piece of machinery
		The crews of the ships reported for duty. There are three crews to each crane so that work can go on throughout the day and night.
cruise	....	to sail from port to port in a ship
		During her fortnight's cruise, the ship called at many places.

cue	....	previous speaker's words so that an actor knows when to speak; stick used in billiards Learn your cues so that you know when to enter. He chalked the end of his cue.
Kew	....	Botanical gardens outside London Go down to Kew in lilac time!
queue	....	long line of people I joined the bus queue.
currant	....	a small dried grape She put currants and raisins into the fruit cake.
current	....	running water, air etc.; electricity passing through wires; of the present, tendency (of opinions etc.) The ocean's currents play a large part in navigation. Turn off the current before leaving the office. This is the current edition of the directory. The current of opinion in the board room is for automation.
cymbal	....	brass musical instrument The cymbals crashed loudly.
symbol	....	conventional sign Two fishes were an early symbol of Christianity.

dear or deer?

dear	....	expensive; loved Diamonds are dear. His wife was very dear to him.
deer	....	a horned ruminant There are deer in the New Forest.
demean	....	to lower oneself Do not demean yourself by squabbling.
demesne	....	land of a manor The lord's demesne provided the household with food.
dependant	....	one who relies on another for support Income tax allowances are made for dependants.
dependent	....	relying on, subject to Children are dependent on their parents for many years. The fete will be held tomorrow, dependent on the weather.

descent	....	route down
		The descent of a mountain can be as difficult as the ascent.
dissent	....	disagree; non-conformity
		His dissent meant that the decision was not unanimous. The dissent of the Methodists established a new Church.
dew	....	precipitation of water, especially at dusk
		Cobwebs are often covered with dew in autumn.
due	....	owing; adequate; exactly
		The bills fall due half-yearly. He received his due reward. The plane flew due east.
die (dying)	....	to give up life
		His father is dying.
dye (dyeing)	....	change colour by using chemicals
		I am going to dye the blue curtains red.
draft	....	rough copy; written order for money; group of men chosen from a larger body for special duty
		A fair copy was made from his draft to give to the press. Get a draft on the bank to pay the merchants. A draft has been sent from London to reinforce the Brighton police.
draught	....	a current of air; depth of water required to float a ship
		Close the door, there is a draught. The draught of the *Queen Mary* is too great to allow her to enter this port.
dual	....	double
		The caravan serves a dual purpose, as a home and for travelling.
duel	....	fight between two people
		There is a duel between the two bidders for the company.

earnest or Ernest?

earnest	....	serious; urgent; proof of
		He is an earnest young man and works hard. We are sending the goods today at their earnest request. He has paid the deposit in earnest of his intentions to buy.
Ernest	....	forename
		May I introduce Mr Ernest Montmorency?
eruption	....	a bursting out
		The eruption of Vesuvius destroyed Pompei.
irruption	....	violent entry
		An irruption of gate-crashers ruined the party.

faint or feint?

faint	....	lose consciousness
		The girl fainted when she saw the accident.
feint	....	pretend to attack
		The boxer feinted to get beneath his opponent's guard.
fair	....	blonde; just; a regular gathering for markets etc.
		She has fair hair. One should give a fair day's work for a fair day's wage. There are always amusements at the midsummer fair.
fare	....	price paid for a journey, etc.; food
		You must pay your fare on the railway. Foreign fare is often exotic to English taste.
fate	....	destiny
		He sealed his fate when he forgot to deliver the message.
fete	....	festival
		The fifteenth of August is a fete day in many countries.
feat	....	achievement
		Amundsen's journey to the South Pole was a great feat of endurance.
feet	....	plural of foot
		There are three feet in a yard. Centipedes are alleged to have a hundred feet.
fisher	....	one who fishes
		The lobster fisher laid his pots in the bay.
fissure	....	a split
		The fissures in the glacier impeded the climbers.
flair	....	talent
		Because she has a flair for business, the shop is doing well.
flare	....	flame up quickly
		Cottons are dangerous for children's clothes because they flare easily. His temper flared up as he read the report.
flour	....	ground-up grain, roots, etc.
		Bakers make bread from wheat-flour.
flower	....	reproductive part of plants
		Flowers are brightly coloured to attract insects for pollination.

for	....	preposition He stayed for a month. We went for a walk. He is member for this area. Please buy it for me. For all you say it is not so.
fore	....	in front, ready The bows are the fore part of the ship. He went in the fore-noon. The new man came to the fore during the crisis.
four	....	number 'One, two, three, four,' counted the little boy.
forgo	....	to go without, to relinquish The President agreed to forgo his privileges.
forego	....	to go before in place or time I shall be pleased to receive your comments on the foregoing information.
formally	....	what is required by custom or usage They were formally introduced by the toastmaster.
formerly	....	previously The new secretary was formerly in the typing pool.
forth	....	Scottish river mouth; out Edinburgh stands on the Firth of Forth. The raiding party sallied forth from the castle.
fourth	....	ordinal number There were prizes for the first three, but he came fourth.
foul	....	dirty; loathsome The old house was foul with cobwebs. The tramp was a foul object.
fowl	....	bird They get eggs from their fowls.
freeze	....	turn to ice or cover with ice We will freeze a lot of raspberries in the summer.
frieze	....	band of decoration There was a patterned frieze between the wall and ceiling in the dining-room.
fir	....	coniferous tree Firs are grown for pit props.
fur	....	hairy growth on animals Mink is a very expensive fur.

gait or gate?

gait	....	manner of walking You can tell by his gait that he is flat-footed.
gate	....	barrier closing the opening in a wall The park gate shuts at sunset.
gamble	....	play games of chance for money, bet on races; take a risk Many people gamble on football pools.
gambol	....	frisk Lambs gambol over the moors in the spring.
gilt	....	decorated with gold Old books often have gilt letters for their titles.
guilt	....	having committed an offence Their guilt was obvious because they still had the stolen goods.
gaol/jail	....	prison (either spelling: gaol on official documents, jail in America)
gorilla	....	large, wild ape The gorilla robbed the orchard in Africa.
guerilla	....	independent soldiers The army had withdrawn but the invaders had to suffer guerilla attacks.
great	....	large; famous; important Westminster Abbey is a great building. Roosevelt was a great man. The coronation was a great occasion.
grate	....	hearth A coal fire in the grate is cheerful.

hail or hale?

hail	....	shout a greeting; tiny balls of ice; pour down They hail the ship. Hail fell steadily all day. Curses hailed down on the attackers.
hale	....	healthy He is back after his illness, as hale and hearty as ever.
hair	....	fine filaments growing from the skin She has a head of thick golden hair.
hare	....	a small rodent The hare goes mad in March.

hall	....	entrance to a building; place for large assemblies The umbrella stand is in the hall. They hired the village hall for the party.
haul	....	pull; amount gained The men must haul on the rope together. The burglar's haul was worth thousands of pounds.
heal	....	cure He knew how to heal the blind.
heel	....	back of the foot; back of a shoe, stocking; lean over because of the wind or uneven load. There was a hole in the heel of his sock. The load slipped and the lorry heeled over.
hear	....	receive with the ear I can hear the birds singing.
here	....	in this place I put it here on my desk.
heard	....	past tense of 'hear' I heard a bird on the roof.
herd	....	group of cattle, etc. The herd of cows lay in the shade.
heir	....	next in line to property or position when the present holder dies or retires He is heir to his father's lands.
air	....	the atmosphere surrounding the earth All rooms should have a supply of fresh air.
higher	....	further up Peter is higher on the path than Paul.
hire	....	pay rent for borrowing Many people prefer to hire a television set rather than buy one.
hoard	....	collect and put away Most of us hoard useless objects in our houses.
horde	....	unruly mob There was a vast horde of children in the toy department.
hoarse	....	rough-voiced Most people are hoarse when they have a cold.
horse	....	an animal The horse was the only means of transport for many centuries.

hole	....	hollow place in a solid
		There was a hole in the bag and the sugar ran out.
whole	....	complete; perfect
		The jigsaw was whole. The whole tea-set was very valuable.
holy	....	sacred
		Jerusalem is a holy place for Christians, Jews and Moslems.
wholly	....	completely
		The letter was wholly unnecessary.
hour	....	unit of time, containing sixty minutes
		We waited an hour, from ten to eleven.
our	....	adjective, belonging to us
		We have just bought our first car.

idle or idol?

idle	....	without work
		The machinery has been idle for the last six months.
idol	....	statue of a god that is worshipped; person or thing that receives an extreme degree of adoration
		Primitive peoples made idols for the temples. Valentino was the idol of early filmgoers.
I'll	....	contraction of 'I shall' or 'I will' (emphatic future)
		I'll go now. I'll go, in spite of what you say.
isle	....	a small area of land surrounded by water (often poetic)
		'This sceptered isle . . . England, bound in with the triumphant sea.'
aisle	....	passages between seats in a church or place of public entertainment
		The usherette showed them to their seats next to the aisle.
incidence	....	range; falling on
		The incidence of many diseases has been reduced by the World Health Organisation.
incidents	....	events
		The incidents in the plot were very plausible.

incite	....	stir up, often rebellion The orator incited the crowd to lynch the man.
insight	....	see into someone's mind or character He showed great insight and understanding when dealing with the personnel.

jam or jamb?

jail/gaol	....	prison (either spelling; gaol on official documents, jail in American)
jam	....	block; become wedged; fruit preserved by boiling with sugar The road was jammed with traffic. The machine jammed and work had to stop. There was strawberry jam for tea.
jamb	....	side post of a door, window or fireplace The jambs were made of marble.

key or quay?

key	....	piece of metal used to turn the wards in a lock You need a key to unlock that door.
quay	....	artificial wall for ships to be tied up to There were five boats tied to the quay and many more anchored in the harbour.
Kew	....	botanical gardens outside London Go down to Kew in lilac time!
queue	....	long line of people I joined the bus queue.
cue	....	previous speaker's words so that an actor knows when to speak; stick used in billiards Learn your cues so that you know when to enter. He chalked the end of his cue.
knead	....	make a dough of flour and water The baker kneads the bread before it is baked.
need	....	want; necessity; require Many children are in need these days. We need food for life. The typewriter needs cleaning.
knew	....	past tense of 'know' She knew how to type.
new	....	first made or invented or possessed It is new bread. This has a new system of fuel injection. My new car is a secondhand Ford.

knight	....	rank or title (originally military) Sir Ernest Smith is a Knight of the Thistle.
night	....	period of time from sunset to sunrise Nights are short in summer.
know	....	understand; recognise I know how to solve the problem. Do you know Mr Brown?
no	....	negative There is no more paper. No, I have not finished the typing.

lead or led?

lead	....	base metal Lead is used in roofing and by plumbers.
led	....	past tense of 'to lead' The path led past the lake.
lessen	....	decrease Aspirins will lessen the pain.
lesson	....	systematic instruction She is taking driving lessons.
licence	....	permission A licence is necessary to sell stamps.
license,-ce	....	to grant permission (There is no rule about -se or -ce, the former being the more usual.) Innkeepers are licensed to sell beer.
lightening	....	to make lighter By sharing the work, we are lightening the load.
lightning	....	flash of electricity in the sky The house was struck by lightning.
lie	....	to have one's body in a horizontal position; to tell an untruth After lunch, he lies down for an hour. The child lied about the broken window.
lye	....	strong alkaline solution for washing Lye is delivered in bulk to laundries.

literal	....	written; exactly following the original; taking the primary meaning of words
		He submitted a literal report. This is a literal translation of the German. Be careful what you say because children take the literal meaning of your words.
littoral	....	Region lying along shore or coastline
		From the boat we could see the littoral.
loan	....	grant temporary use of something
		The book is on loan from the public library for a fortnight.
lone	....	solitary, alone
		The lone flyer crossed the Atlantic.
loath	....	unwilling
		The child was loath to do his homework.
loathe	....	hate, detest
		Most of us loathe the cold and snow.
lumbar	....	of the back
		He had a pain in his lumbar region.
lumber	....	rough, cut, timber; rubbish
		In Canada, lumber is floated down the rivers. The attic was full of unused furniture and other lumber.

made or maid?

made	....	formed, shaped; acquired
		The model was made of bronze. He made a thousand pounds on the deal.
maid	....	female servant
		The maid was clearing the hotel bedroom.
magnate	....	wealthy or eminent man
		There are many oil magnates in Texas.
magnet	....	metal with the property of attracting other metals
		A magnet is very useful for picking up split pins.
mail	....	post; form of armour
		The Royal Mail carried letters and parcels. Chain mail was worn by soldiers in the twelfth century.
male	....	of the masculine sex
		All male members of the staff will report at nine o'clock and female members at ten.

mare	....	female horse
		The mare and her foal were grazing in the field.
mayor	....	first citizen of a borough
		The mayor presided at the council meetings.
marshal	....	high rank in some armies; arrange in correct order
		The marshal inspected the army. Please marshal all the facts for the next meeting of the board.
martial	....	of warfare
		Martial law is much more severe than civilian law.
mean	....	close-fisted; skimpy; average
		To become a miser, you must be very mean. Don't be mean with the fruit in your next cake. The mean annual temperature of the islands is 80° F.
mien	....	bearing, air
		Elizabeth thought Mr Darcy proud because of his mien.
meat	....	flesh of an animal used for eating
		That butcher sells good meat.
meet	....	encounter
		The directors meet every Monday.
mete	....	give out
		The courts mete out justice.
medal	....	piece of metal struck to commemorate an event; award to soldiers etc. for gallantry
		The medal of Malta's George Cross is in the museum at Valletta.
meddle	....	interfere
		Never meddle in matters you do not understand.
metal	....	substances like gold, silver, lead
		Saucepans are made of various metals.
mettle	....	courage, ardour
		The new contract has put the workers on their mettle to produce the goods before their rivals.
mews	....	stables enclosing an open yard
		Many of the mews in London have been converted into dwellings.
muse	....	ponder deeply; one of the nine goddesses of the Arts
		The poet muses on his verses. Terpsichore is the Muse of dancing.

miner	....	underground worker
		The coal miner works at the coal face.
minor	....	trivial; under age
		The paper clips were a minor detail in the schedule. In Britain, you are a minor until you are eighteen.
missed	....	past tense of 'miss
		The party arrived too late and missed their train.
mist	....	fine water vapour
		Mist rises from the marshes in autumn.

naval or navel?

naval	....	of the navy
		Naval officers serve in the ships of the Royal Navy.
navel	....	a depression in the body left by the severance of the umbilical cord
		The navel orange is so called because it has a depression at the top which resembles a navel.
nay	....	no
		Let your yea by yea, and your nay, nay.
née	....	born
		Mrs Smith, née Carter, opened the fete.
neigh	....	noise made by a horse
		The horses neigh for lumps of sugar.
need	....	want; require
		Many children are in need these days. The typewriter needs cleaning.
knead	....	work a dough of flour and water
		The baker kneads the bread before it is baked.
new	....	first made or invented or possessed
		It is new bread. This has a new system of fuel injection. My new car is a secondhand Ford.
knew	....	past tense of 'know'
		She knew how to type.
night	....	period of time from sunset to sunrise
		Nights are short in summer.
knight	....	rank or title (originally military)
		Sir Ernest Smith is a Knight of the Thistle.

no	....	negative
		There is no more paper. No, I have not finished the typing.
know	....	understand; recognise
		I know how to solve the problem. Do you know Mr Brown?

oar, ore or or?

oar	....	shaped piece of wood for propelling a boat
		A gondola is propelled by a single oar.
or	....	introduces the second of two alternatives
		Shall we take the stairs or the lift?
ore	....	rock from which metal is extracted
		The iron-ore comes from Spain to the smelting works.
our	....	adjective, belonging to us
		We have just bought our first car.
hour	....	unit of time; containing sixty minutes
		We waited an hour from ten to eleven.

packed or pact?

packed	....	filled up; pushed tightly in
		The trunks are packed. The crowd packed the hall to hear him speak.
pact	....	treaty
		The two nations signed a pact of friendship.
pail	....	buckets
		There was a pail in the dinghy for bailing out the boat.
pale	....	faintly coloured; fence
		The room was painted very pale blue. A wooden pale enclosed the garden.
pain	....	ache
		The boy had a pain where his shoe pinched.
pane	....	sheet of glass
		The picture window was a large pane of plate-glass.

pair	....	set of two He bought a new pair of shoes.
pare	....	peel thinly; cut down little by little There is a special knife to pare potatoes. We must pare running expenses to the minimum.
pear	....	fruit of the pear tree Doyen de Comice is the finest pear on the market.
passed	....	past tense of 'pass' He passed the shop an hour ago. The information was passed on to the manager.
past	....	of time; of place He walked past the shop an hour ago. It is past ten o'clock. The house is just past the corner.
patience	....	endurance of suffering; calmness under strain With great patience, he learnt to walk again. Mothers need patience to deal with children.
patients	....	sick people attending surgeries, hospitals etc. for treatment The doctor saw fifty patients this morning.
peace	....	freedom from war Most of the world is now at peace.
piece	....	a segment of something Put a new piece of paper in the typewriter. Cut a piece of cake.
peak	....	top The peak of the mountain broke through the clouds. The man is at the peak of his profession.
peek	....	peer round Neighbours peek round the curtains to see what is going on.
pique	....	annoyance; irritate; arouse He burned the documents in a fit of pique. Bores pique one. His reticence piqued my curiosity.
peal	....	bells rung in a rhythmic pattern Church bells peal out on Sunday mornings.
peel	....	remove the skin Some people peel the apples before eating them.
pedal	....	foot lever Some cars have two pedals, foot-brake and accelerator.
peddle	....	sell in small quantities, usually from door to door Kleen-e-ze men peddle brushes for a living.

peer	....	look round stealthily; member of the House of Lord's; one's equal
		They peer round the door to see who rings. Earl Blank is a peer. Shakespeare has no peer as a dramatist.
pier	....	structure running out into the sea, used for promenades and also moorings
		Southend pier has a café at the end.
plain	....	simple; flat country
		The wall was covered with plain paint. The village stood in the centre of the plain.
plane	....	tool for smoothing wood; short for aeroplane
		The plane smoothed the rough timber. The plane left for Paris at mid-day.
plum	....	fruit with a sweet pulp and a flattish stone
		The Victoria plum is sweet to eat.
plumb	....	ball of lead that helps to ensure vertical building, etc.
		The mason checked the wall with his plumb-line.
pole	....	long piece of wood, metal, etc.
		The flag pole stood 80 feet high.
poll	....	vote
		At a general election all voters go to the poll.
poor	....	needy; inadequate; insignificant
		They were too poor to buy food. Their poor clothing did not keep them warm. 'A poor thing but mine own.'
pore	....	opening in the skin
		We perspire through our pores.
pour	....	to make liquid flow; flow of words
		They pour out tea. The words poured forth.
practice	....	(n) custom; repeated actions to learn; professional work
		It is our practice to do the letters before four o'clock. Practice makes perfect. That dentist has a large practice.
practise	....	(v) Practise finishing the letters before four o'clock
		You must practise your typing. The dentist practises in London.

pray	....	beseech; beg God or a person In some countries they pray for rain.
prey	....	animal killed for food by another The lion stalked its prey across the veld.
principal	....	chief The principal officers of the company met yesterday.
principle	....	code of moral conduct It is against my principles to steal.
presence	....	mien His presence was enough to overawe one.
presents	....	gifts 'Unbirthday' presents are the nicest.
profit	....	benefit; be of advantage; gain The business will be to our profit. There is little profit from that branch.
prophet	....	one who foretells the future The prophet warned the people of the Flood but only Noah heeded his words.

quay or key?

quay	....	artificial wall for ships to be tied up to There were five boats tied to the quay and many more anchored in the harbour.
key	....	piece of metal used to turn the wards in a lock You need a key to unlock that door.
queue	....	long line of people I joined the bus queue.
cue	....	previous speaker's words so that an actor knows when to speak; stick used in billiards Learn your cues so that you know when to enter. He chalked the end of his cue.
Kew	....	botanical gardens outside London Go down to Kew in lilac time!
quire	....	24 sheets of writing paper; any number of bound leaves in a book Poor typists need a quire of paper for one letter.
choir	....	a group of singers Vocal works performed at the Promenade concerts often require a large choir.

rain, rein or reign?

rack	....	framework with rails and bars; instrument of torture
		The paper is stored on racks. The prisoner was stretched on the rack.
wrack	....	seaweed, etc. washed ashore
		They collected wrack on the shore to send to the fertilizer factory.
rain	....	precipitation of water
		The amount of rain is measured in inches.
reign	....	rule, hold royal office
		The civil war took place during the reign of Charles I.
rein	....	part of the bridle of a horse
		The reins enable the rider to control the bit in the horse's mouth.
raise	....	lift; grow
		Cranes raise the materials to the top of the building. Nurserymen raise plants.
rays	....	beams of light
		The rays of the sun lit the room.
raze, -se	....	completely destroy
		The city was razed to the ground.
rap	....	smack sharply
		I'll rap your knuckles for disobedience.
wrap	....	enclose or pack in enfolding material
		Wrap up warmly in the snow. Please wrap up this parcel.
read	....	past tense of 'to read'
		He read that book last year.
red	....	a colour
		Bulls dislike red.
read	....	turn symbols into meaning
		He can read Arabic.
reed	....	plant
		Reeds grow by water and in marshy ground.

real	....	actual; true
		The ring is real gold. These are the real facts.
reel	....	spool for thread; dance
		The cotton is on a wooden reel. Scots and Irish dance the reel.
rest	....	repose
		Holidays are a rest from work.
wrest	....	seize violently
		The detective wrested the knife from the youth.
right	....	correct; proper
		The right answer to 3 plus 4 is 7. It is the right thing to reply to invitations at once.
rite	....	usual action in religious or solemn ceremonies
		Human sacrifice was an ancient rite.
wright	....	skilled worker
		He trained as a shipwright.
write	....	put down symbols for sounds
		Authors write books.
ring	....	sound of bells
		Peals of bells ring out on Sundays.
wring	....	twist, squeeze
		Wring the clothes before hanging them out to dry.
road	....	highway
		Cars drive on the road.
rode	....	past tense of 'to ride'
		The huntsman rode a brown horse.
rowed	....	past tense and past participle of verb 'to row'
		The crew rowed well and won the race.
role	....	part
		The actor had the principal role in *Hamlet*.
roll	....	turn over and over
		I saw the coin roll under the table.
rote	....	learnt by repetition
		Multiplication tables are learnt by rote.
wrote	....	past tense of 'to write'
		Dickens wrote many novels.

sail or sale?

sail	....	cloth which catches the wind to drive a ship, etc.
		The yacht spread her sail.
sale	....	exchange of goods for money
		He is licensed for the sale of postage stamps.

scene	....	section of a play; display of temper
		The first scene was set in a garden. The child made a scene when she could not have her own way.
seen	....	past part. of 'to see'
		He was last seen on the platform at Waterloo.
sea	....	salt water surrounding the coasts
		The North Sea is a potential oil field.
see	....	interpret with the eyes or mind
		I can see the bus coming. We can see the point of his argument.
sealing	....	securing with wax, etc.; placing a seal on a document, in addition to a signature, to show that the document is genuine.
		The sealing of the contract took place in front of four witnesses.
ceiling	....	the top of a room; the top price, wages; highest level of flights, etc.
		The new plane flies at a ceiling of 75,000 feet.
seam	....	line where two edges join
		The zip was set in the back seam of the dress. There was a seam in the wallpaper.
seem	....	appear
		They are cleverer than they seem.
seed	....	the part of the fruit of a plant that grows into a new plant
		He spent Sunday afternoons sewing gardenia seeds.
cede	....	yield
		Gibraltar was ceded by Spain to Britain many years ago.
sell	....	to find purchasers for goods, property, etc.
		Co-operatives sell many kinds of merchandise.
cell	....	small room in a monastery or prison; smallest living unit
		The amoeba is a single-cell animal.
seller	....	one who sells
		The seller made a profit of a pound on the deal.
cellar	....	space under a building, often used for storage
		Coal used to be shot into the cellar.

scent	....	a pleasant smell; the smell of an animal Women love French scent. The hounds follow the scent of the fox.
sent	....	past tense of 'to send' The goods were sent yesterday.
cent	....	division of a hundred A cent is one hundredth part of a dollar. Interest is quoted at so much per cent.
serial	....	part of a series; narrative published in instalments Many magazines publish serial stories which run for several issues.
cereal	....	grain crops The cereal crops of North America are wheat and maize.
serge	....	weave of fabric He was wearing a blue serge suit.
surge	....	sudden rising up The tidal wave caused a surge of water up the coast.
session	....	uninterrupted period of time for the discussion of business The board was in session for five hours on Monday to discuss the new factory.
cession	....	surrendering rights in property or land The cession of Hong Kong to Britain gave the British a port in China.
sew	....	stitch She sews a fine seam.
so	....	conjunction expressing consequence It was fine so we went for a stroll in the sun.
sow	....	plant seeds Farmers sow wheat in winter.
shear	....	cut the wool off sheep Farmers shear their sheep in spring.
sheer	....	perpendicularly; thin The cliff fell sheer into the sea. Chiffon is a sheer fabric.
sight	....	ability to see; a spectacle Engine drivers must have good sight. The Lord Mayor's Show is a sight to remember.
site	....	ground on which a building or town stands. The new factory site is just outside Glasgow.

cite	....	to quote
		lawyers often cite precedents in court.
soar	....	rise
		Larks soar into the sky.
sore	....	painful
		A sprained ankle is sore.
sole	....	only
		He was the sole survivor of the shipwreck.
soul	....	spirit
		The soul is the immortal part of Man.
some	....	a certain quantity of
		I need some more paper.
sum	....	total
		The sum of 7 plus 9 plus 5 is 21.
stairs	....	treads and risers to form a way up
		There are three flights of stairs in the building.
stares	....	gazes intently
		He stares all day at the television screen.
stake	....	share, often in a gamble; post, pillar
		He has a stake in the business. There was a metal stake for the washing line.
steak	....	cut of beef
		They all ate steak and chips.
stationary	....	not moving
		The bus was stationary at the terminus.
stationery	....	writing materials
		Please add carbons to the stationery order.
steal	....	take what does not belong to one
		Burglars steal money.
steel	....	alloys of iron and carbon
		Stainless steel is used for many purposes.
sterling	....	of solid worth; area of world currency
		He does sterling work for the company. The stability of sterling is important in world trade.
Stirling	....	Scottish town
		Stirling has an ancient castle.

stile	....	steps over a fence or hedge for pedestrians The old stile gave access to the field path.
style	....	fashion; manner This dress is the latest style. He has an unusual style of writing.
straight	....	without curves or corners Roman roads ran straight across the countryside.
strait	....	narrow strip of water; puritanical The Straits of Gibraltar connect the Atlantic with the Mediterranean. They are too strait-laced to go to the theatre.
suite	....	matching furniture etc.; group of rooms There was a settee and three armchairs in the suite. He hired a suite of rooms in the hotel.
sweet	....	tasting of sugar Many people do not like sweet tea.
symbol	....	conventional sign Two fishes were an early symbol of Christianity.
cymbal	....	brass musical instrument The cymbals crashed loudly.

tail or tale?

tail	....	hind end The dog wags his tail.
tale	....	story Children love a bed-time tale.
tares	....	weeds Good crops should be free of tares.
tears	....	partial breaks There are tears in the paper.
taught	....	past tense of 'to teach' He taught at the local school.
taut	....	fully stretched Pull the string round the parcel taut.
tort	....	private or civil or criminal wrong 'Tort' is a legal term meaning a breach of a duty imposed by law.
team	....	a side, especially in ball games The town football team has had a winning season.
teem	....	pour down; overflow It is teeming with rain. The streets teem with people on Bank Holiday.

tear	....	drop of water from the eye A tear ran down her cheek.
tier	....	layer The cake had three tiers. The seats were arranged in tiers.
there	....	in that place Put it there.
their	....	belonging to them It is their responsibility, not ours.
they're	....	Short for 'they are' They're at home now.
threw	....	past tense of 'to throw' He threw the javelin in the 1972 Olympics.
through	....	from end to end; from side to side; because of He searched through the drawers. It was through his action that the child was saved.
tide	....	regular movements of water; carry over The rise and fall of the tide is due to the attraction of the sun and moon. We have enough business to tide us over the next few months.
tied	....	past tense of 'to tie' The bow was well tied.
tire	....	to weary; band of metal etc. on a wheel Bores tire one out. I am tired of hearing about his adventure. The car needs a new spare tire.
tyre	....	alternative spelling for tire—band on a wheel.
to	....	towards; as far as; comparisons; recipients Turn left off the road to London. Go to the church and turn left. I prefer green to yellow. I gave it to him.
too	....	excess; also Do not speak too loudly. There are too many people. He came too.
two	....	number She wrote one or two letters.
toe	....	small limb at end of foot; part of shoe The ballerina danced on her toes. He trod on the toe of my shoe.
tow	....	pull The tugs tow the ship out of harbour.

tracked	....	followed clues The hunter tracked down the lion by its spoor.
tract	....	a stretch of land; writing with a purpose A vast tract of desert lay in front of them. Many Churches publish tracts to explain their teachings.
trait	....	characteristic Loyalty is an excellent trait in an employee.
tray	....	flat vessel for carrying small articles The cups and saucers were carried on a tray.
treaties	....	plural of 'treaty' Nations sign treaties of friendship with each other.
treatise	....	learned essay on a subject The historian wrote a treatise on Napoleon.
troop	....	detachment of soldiers, etc.; flock together The captain led his troop into battle. The children trooped to the funfair.
troupe	....	company of actors, etc. The circus troupe led the parade.

vain, vein or vane?

vain	....	conceited She is very vain of her hands.
vane	....	weathercock The vane on the church tower shows an east wind.
vein	....	major blood vessel in the body; mood The veins carry blood to the heart. He spoke in a humorous vein at the party.
vial	....	small glass vessel for holding liquids He gave her a vial of perfume.
vile	....	loathsome; despicable, foul-tasting His treatment of the child was vile. The medicine tasted vile.

waist or waste?

waist	....	part of human body below ribs and above hips She wore a belt round her waist.
waste	....	refuse All waste paper should go in the bin provided.

wait	....	stay until some expected event occurs You must wait here for the bus.
weight	....	heaviness The weight of the new safe is 5 cwt.
waive	....	forgo a claim He waived his right to compensation.
wave	....	ridge and trough movement of a liquid The wind raised waves on the sea.
wares	....	goods made for sale Stallholders cry their wares.
wears	....	has on; damage by rubbing or use He wears a kilt. She wears her shoes out very quickly.
way	....	road; means The best way is by the high street. In what way can we help?
weigh	....	find the weight of; consider all sides of a problem Weigh yourself on the scales. We must weigh up all the pros and cons before we decide.
weak	....	feeble The old lady was weak with age. His excuses are very weak.
week	....	seven days It will take a week, so call in next Friday.
weather	....	atmospheric conditions Poor weather spoils a holiday.
whether	....	introduces an alternative I don't know whether he received the message. They will stay whether he comes or not.
wet	....	moistened Rain makes the garden wet.
whet	....	stimulate; sharpen His few remarks whet my appetite for more information. The butcher whetted his knife before cutting the meat.
which	....	asking for a choice; conjunction Which of these books do you prefer? The cat which ran along the road belongs to that house.
witch	....	a woman practising magic A witch was burned at the stake.

whole	....	complete, perfect
		The jigsaw was whole. The whole tea-set was very valuable.
hole	....	hollow place in a solid
		There was a hole in the bag and sugar ran out.
wholly	....	completely
		The letter was wholly unnecessary.
holy	....	sacred
		Jerusalem is a holy place for Christians, Jews and Moslems.
who's	....	short form for 'who is' or 'who has'
		The man who's just come in is Mr Perkins.
whose	....	shows possession
		The man whose car is outside is my neighbour.
wood	....	part of a tree; group of trees
		The furniture is made of wood. We picnicked in a small wood.
would	....	want, desire
		They would like to go to the zoo.
wrack	....	seaweed, etc. washed ashore
		They collected wrack on the shore to send to the manure factory.
rack	....	framework with rails and bars; instrument of torture
		The paper is stored on racks. The prisoner was stretched on the rack.
wrap	....	enclose or pack in enfolding material
		Wrap up warmly in the snow. Please wrap up this parcel.
rap	....	smack snarply
		I'll rap you knuckles for disobedience.
wrest	....	seize violently
		The detective wrested the knife from the youth.
rest	....	repose
		Holidays are a rest from work.
wright	....	skilled worker
		He trained as a shipwright.
write	....	put down symbols for sounds
		Authors write books.

right	....	correct, proper
		The right answer to 3 plus 4 is 7. It is the right thing to reply to invitations at once.
rite	....	usual action in religious or solemn ceremonies
		Human sacrifice was an ancient rite.
wring	....	twist, squeeze
		Wring the clothes before hanging them out to dry.
ring	....	sound of bells
		Peals of bells ring out on Sundays.
wrote	....	past tense of 'to write'
		Dickens wrote many novels.
rote	....	learnt by repetition
		Multiplication tables are learnt by rote.

yolk or yoke?

yolk	....	yellow centre of an egg
		Only the yolk of the egg is used for mayonnaise.
yoke	....	tie together; piece of wood fastened over the necks of animals; part of clothing over the shoulders
		Farmers yoke oxen to pull carts. A bell swung from the yoke of the horses at the plough. The shirt has a deep yoke at the back.
your	....	belong to you
		Have you had your holiday yet?
you're	....	short form of 'you are'
		I hear you're going on holiday soon.

EXERCISES

Write or type the following sentences, choosing the correct words from those in brackets.

1 (a) (Ernest, earnest) who was acting the part of the (heir, air) forgot his (Kew, queue, cue).
 (b) (Your, you're) (ore, or, oar) lay (idol, idle) on the rowlocks.
 (c) The (magnate, magnet) ran and (caught, court) the (stationary, stationery) bus.
 (d) He was (loath, loathe) to pass through the (wood, would) because of the (bare, bear).

(e) There was (formally, formerly) a (vane, vain, vein) on the (peak, peek, pique) of the steeple.
(f) (Their, there, they're) sitting in a (draft, draught) coming (threw, through) the (jam, jamb) of the door.
(g) You (knew, new) by his (mean, mien) that he would (cede, seed) his rights.
(h) The (quire, choir) (wares, wears) (grate, great) white cassocks.
(i) (Aid, aide) was (kneaded, needed) after the (irruption, eruption) of the volcano.
(j) (Your, you're) plans are (dependant, dependent) on the (naval, navel) strength of the country.

2 (a) The (rays, raze, raise) of the sun came through the (whole, hole) in the (beach, beech) fence.
(b) His (feat, feet) were in a (vial, vile) state from (lead, led) poisoning.
(c) (Hour, our) (presence, presents) included a (yolk, yoke) for the oxen.
(d) He (sited, cited, sighted) the (incidence, incidents) as an example of (shear, sheer) folly.
(e) They (rote, wrote) of lambs (gambling, gambolling) in the April (missed, mist.)
(f) Is (already, all ready) (for, fore, four) the (practice, practise)?
(g) He is well known for his (treaties, treatise) on the (demean, demesne) tenure of (knights, nights).
(h) I (heard, herd) the (bridal, bridle) (rains, reigns, reins) were gold.
(i) The (assistance, assistants) waited at the (gait, gate) to the (key, quay).
(j) We (know, no) that his (incite, insight) took him (strait, straight) to the heart of the problems.

3 (a) They had to (higher, hire) (canvas, canvass) for the (wring, ring).
(b) The (boarder, border) had a (flair, flare) for buying valuable (lumber, lumbar).
(c) The legs of the (dual, duel) purpose (trait, tray) (packed, pact) neatly away.
(d) The assayer (made, maid) the (sole, soul) (check, cheque) on the (metal, mettle).
(e) We (aught, ought) to (way, weigh) up the evidence before we decide on his (gilt, guilt).
(f) There are (dear, deer) (hear, here) (to, too, two).
(g) We (read, reed) that the (borough, burrow) agreed to make a (loan, lone) to the civic theatre.
(h) The (gorillas, guerrillas) jumped (altogether, all together) over the (fishers, fissures) in the glacier.
(i) The (stairs, stares) leading to the (hall, haul) were covered in (dew, due).
(j) '(Aisle, isle, I'll) (toe, tow) another (arc, ark) if there isn't room in this,' said Noah.

4 If you chose the wrong homophone in any of these sentences, make up your own sentence for the wrongly-used one.
   e.g. The (ascent, assent) was difficult.
        The assent of the mountain was difficult. .... wrong answer.
        The assent of all the meeting meant unanimous agreement to the plan. .... your correction.

5 Explain briefly the differences in meaning between each of the following pairs:
   (a) allowed, aloud; nay, neigh; tide, tied; male, mail; cent, scent.
   (b) berry, bury; hoarse, horse; waist, waste; fair, fare; lessen, lesson.
   (c) cheap, cheep; peer, pier; altar, alter; some, sum; tail, tale.
   (d) die, dye; board, bored; hair, hare; rest, wrest; lightening, lightning.
   (e) miner, minor; flour, flower; chews, choose; troop, troupe; stake, steak.

6 Correct the following sentences, where necessary:
   (a) 'Awl bale, then I am confident that our fete will not be to drown', shouted the captain.
   (b) The hoard ran down to the literal plane.
   (c) The core of correspondence caste the complacent cruise into the currant.
   (d) He decided to wave the prophet on the plumb pudding for orphanage.
   (e) Please by sum serge for your new coat.

7 (a) The dissent of the bolder-strewn mountainside was difficult.
   (b) The chord ran across the real out to seeff
   (c) The barren balled at the buoy for breaking the bre.
   (d) He tort geography here last cession.
   (e) Last week's whether was whet.

8 (a) The counsel meats in the town hall.
   (b) I'm sorry, we have no bred, only roles.
   (c) The principle pedalled a pare of pails with great patients.
   (d) I could not read the cymbal on the wait.
   (e) The martial won a meddle for bravery.

9 (a) The read ribbon fell on the rode.
   (b) The compare paid a complement to the artist.
   (c) The suite sale of the ship stole the seen.
   (d) The cannon walked across the Close to his sell.
   (e) The teem had a license to fish the river.

10 (a) His heal court on the style.
   (b) The which stalked her pray over the course grass.
   (c) The fur tree stood fourth in the fowl freizing fog.
   (d) The caret dangled from the choler of the donkey.
   (e) The bowled man took the sugar-beat from the barn.

11 Correct the following narrative passages:
   (a) The analyst records in his calender that the monks gave arms. The attendants at the seller door of the monastery was greatest on feast days. The holy men swung a censer too rid the Chapter house of the sent of the beggars. On Saints' days, they would poor a little whine into the cups of the mendicants. Then the base voices of the quire would shake the panes of the chapel as a signal that the almoner must close the doors.
   (b) The peace of material was rapped round the child. Later, they wood sew a seem down the back of the garment butt at the moment they were two tyred. Their feat were soar with walking and they had the added burden of carrying the little buoy. As they past the gait of the muse, a pedaller haled them and offered his wears. They shrugged and ran on.
   (c) The town counsellor said that the price of serials did not auger well for the future price of bread. The farmers had not removed the tears from the crops and sow they would have to pay more stirling for foreign wheat. They would have to wrack their brains to find a holy satisfactory solution to the difficulties facing them.
   (d) 'You must not steel the ceiling wax. It makes it very pail and hard to peal.' The girl looked across the courtyard to the staples and saw a troop of players who's cloths were very travell-stained. 'Ah', she thought, 'I must weight till tonight to understand that peace of English.' As she turned to go into the house, she noticed a bare sitting on the boarder of a cloak. It would be an amusing evening finding out about the rolls of the players.
   (e) The special bored meeting was called to consider the descent of one of the directors to the knew plans for the factory. He said that the idea was a waist of stationary and would do nothing to rays the production of the men. The breech of contracts that might result from the changes envisaged by the bored would certainly damage the reputation of the firm.

12 Here are ten words and ten definitions. Pair these off correctly:

   (a) assent   hairy growth on animals
       know   forgo a claim
       vile   endured
       hear   alloys of iron and carbon
       rite   of the back
       dye   expression of agreement
       borne   foul
       lumbar   recognise
       waive   understand through the ear
       steel   change colour by using chemicals
       fur   correct action in solemn ceremonies
   (b) corps   passages between seats in a hall etc.
       mete   sudden rising up
       yolk   foundation

	surge	rope of various thicknesses
	taut	unit of soldiers
	base	born
	due	make a dough
	née	decorated with gold
	aisle	give out
	knead	owing
	cord	fully stretched
	gilt	yellow centre of an egg
(c)	earnest	rough-voiced
	or	statue of a god that is worshipped
	border	proof of
	lone	atmospheric conditions
	vain	showing a desire to act according to someone's wishes
	hoarse	peel thinly
	feint	average
	pare	solitary
	complaisant	introduces second of two alternatives
	mean	proud without reason
	weather	pretend to attack
	idol	edge
(d)	gait	first possessed
	quire	piece of metal used to turn the wards in a lock
	demean	upper limbs of the body of a primate
	new	burst out
	your	systematic instruction
	key	member of the cathedral chapter
	higher	24 sheets of writing paper
	rote	belonging to you
	eruption	lower oneself
	canon	further up
	arms	manner of walking
	lesson	learnt parrot-fashion
(e)	isle	bells rung in rhythmic fashion
	serial	conventional sign
	fore	form of armour
	peal	play games of chance for money
	bye	become wedged
	mail	require
	jam	a small area of land surrounded by water
	tail	thinks over
	gamble	subordinate
	symbol	in front of
	chews	hind end
	need	narrative published in instalments

13 Write the following sentences, inserting the correct words from those suggested in brackets:
   (a) (Its, It's) rusty because it has (laid, lain) out in the rain all night.
   (b) Neither (him, he) nor (I, me) (was, were) much hurt.
   (c) The full (affect, effect) of the storm was not felt because it (past, passed) to the north of the town.
   (d) I know a shopkeeper (whose, who's) (licenced, licensed) to sell tobacco, but not wines and spirits. If he (was, were) to sell them he might (lose, loose) his (licence, license).

14 Explain briefly the differences in use and meaning between the words in each of the following pairs:
   loan, lend; metre, meter; lead, led (same pronunciation); swede, suede; salvage, selvedge.

15 Type *ten sentences* to show that you know *the difference in meaning or use* between the words in each of the following pairs.
   (DO NOT ALTER THE SPELLING)
   (a) lose, loose; (b) laid, lain; (c) affect, effect; (d) imply, infer; (e) emigrant, immigrant; (f) continual, continuous; (g) licence, license; (h) principal, principle; (i) less, fewer; (j) eminent, imminent.

16 Correct the following sentences where necessary:
   (a) The occupiers of the houses in question were present at the luncheon given by the Lord and Lady Mayoress.
   (b) After the press reports of the Public Inquiry James Brown became infamous.
   (c) Having read the metre I am confident that the new heater will prove to be an economic proposition.
   (d) Thank you for your assistance during the passed few weeks.
   (e) Lectures on 'Principals and Practise of Education' will be included in the syllabus.
   (f) I will be twenty-one on 1st June. Will you please make arrangements to issue the license on that date.

17 The office junior hands you the following message:
   Mr. Whites secretary telephoned to say that the practise of ordering weekly supplies of stationary must stop and monthly orders are to be sent instead. The Stock Room will not except orders received later than the first Monday in each month. Section head's are asked to advice each clerk to report if the stock of lose-leaf ledger sheets fall below five hundred. The principle reason for the change is to cut down costs. Re-type the message, making the necessary corrections.

A BARGAIN SALE IS TO CLEAR SURPLUS STOCK

Words Easily Confused—Malapropisms

When words such as *consistency* and *constituency*, which are similar in sound or spelling, are confused with each other they are called malapropisms. The term comes from a play by Sheridan, called *The Rivals*, in which one of the characters, Mrs Malaprop, frequently makes humorous mistakes by using the incorrect word, e.g. 'like an allegory on the banks of the Nile'.

Although malapropisms can be very funny, they are not, of course, acceptable in business letters and written English. Most common malapropisms are listed in this chapter. They form a further group of 'trigger' words, which you must learn so that you avoid making mistakes which could cause you and your company to appear foolish to the recipients of your business communications.

accede or exceed?

accede	....	agree to a request etc.; take up office The directors accede to your request. Deputy chairmen accede to the chair.
exceed	....	do more than permitted; be greater than Do not exceed your duties. His ambitions exceed his abilities.
access	....	entry That door gives access to the corridor.
excess	....	too much An excess of words is called verbiage.

accept	....	agree, receive
		I accept your plant. We often accept presents.
except	....	exclude
		All, except him, were at the meeting. They except the candidates for election from the meeting during voting.
acetic	....	of vinegar
		Pickles are preserved in acetic acid.
aesthetic	....	cultured
		The grand tour led to the aesthetic appreciation of the Acropolis.
ascetic	....	one who practises great self-discipline, austere
		The saint was a true ascetic. His ascetic way of life brought him much admiration.
addition	....	noun from 'to add'
		2 + 2 is an addition. In addition, we visited Paris.
edition	....	form in which books, newspapers etc. are published
		The new edition of *Encyclopaedia Britannica* is due soon. This is the sports edition of the paper.
adapt	....	alter to fit
		We had to adapt the set to suit our stage.
adept	....	skilful
		She is very adept at embroidery and has won many prizes.
adopt	....	take over as one's own
		They adopt my ideas without so much as a 'by your leave'.
adverse	....	hostile
		The yacht fought the adverse winds.
averse	....	unwilling
		She was averse to any new idea.
advice	....	noun
		Take my advice on this matter.
advise	....	verb
		I advise you to try again.

affect	....	pretend to feel, move
		Hypocrites affect sympathy. The sight of her tears affected me greatly.
effect	....	result, bring about
		The effect of his action was felt by everyone. We must effect greater efficiency in the office.
affront	....	insult
		His rude behaviour was an affront to his colleagues.
effrontery	....	insolence
		He had the effrontery to suggest that he was the only person able to understand the problem.
allay	....	pacify
		The surgeon's remarks allay our fears.
alley	....	narrow, mean street
		An alley led behind the houses to the garages.
ally	....	unite, person joined to someone else for a common purpose
		Marriages were used to ally great estates. Russia was our ally in both World Wars.
allusion	....	reference to
		During his speech he made allusion to the company's debt to the retiring chairman.
illusion	....	a wrong idea
		He suffers under the illusion that he is Alexander the Great.
amoral	....	lacking any moral sense
		Many criminals are amoral and do not understand the difference between right and wrong.
immoral	....	against morality, evil
		It is immoral to be cruel to each other.
apposite	....	appropriate
		His amusing speech was very apposite on this occasion.
opposite	....	contrary in position to
		He turned left but the park was in the opposite direction.
appraise	....	estimate the value
		The valuers appraise the estate for probate.
apprise	....	inform
		The papers apprise one of world events.

assay	....	test of precious metals for purity
		There are official offices to assay and stamp gold and silver.
essay	....	composition
		In most exams one has to write an essay.

bouillon or bullion?

bouillon	....	soup
		Bouillon is the French for a thin soup.
bullion	....	bars of precious metal
		Gold bullion is stored at Fort Knox.
breath	....	breeze, air passed through the lungs
		On a hot day, a breath of cool air is refreshing. The dragon's breath was fiery.
breathe	....	drawing breath in and out of lungs
		Dragons breathe fire and smoke.

calendar or calender?

calendar	....	table of dates for a given year
		Hang a calendar by your desk to check the date.
calender	....	steam press for finishing laundry etc.
		The calender smoothed out the wrinkles in the cloth.
colander	....	a bowl with holes for draining
		Put the potatoes in the colander to drain.
capital	....	first city of a country, money invested in industry, commerce etc.
		Vienna, the capital of Austria, is not on the Danube. Invest your capital where it will bring the best interest.
capitol	....	centre of government in ancient Rome
		Americans call their central government offices in Washington D.C. the Capitol.
casual	....	irregular
		Students often do casual work in the vacation.
causal	....	of a cause
		The causal relationship of the events was made clear by the speaker.

cease	....	bring to an end
		Please cease typing whilst I telephone.
seize	....	grab
		I seize every opportunity of getting out into the country.
cemetery	....	burial ground
		There were many headstones in the old cemetery.
symmetry	....	harmony, balance
		The chair spoilt the symmetry of the room. The rose bud gave symmetry to the flower arrangement.
censer	....	incense burner
		Some people use a censer in their homes to perfume the air.
censor	....	one who controls the issuing of plays, books, news etc. on the grounds of morals, sedition, or national expediency.
		All soldiers' letters had to pass the censor during the war.
censure	....	reprove, expression of disapproval
		Parents censure bad behaviour in their children. A vote of censure often brings down a government.
cistern	....	tank for storing water
		A cistern made of plastic cannot burst.
system	....	method of organising
		If you do not have a system you will soon have confusion.
cloths	....	lengths of material
		Cut your coats according to your cloths.
clothes	....	garments
		All clothes start as cloth.
collision	....	impact
		The force of the collision broke her arm.
collusion	....	agreement for wrong purposes
		The gang were in collusion on the warehouse job.
confirm	....	ratify, give support to, settle
		The two Parliaments confirm the treaty. The witnesses confirm the defendant's story. This will confirm his opinion on the matter.
conform	....	adapt oneself to
		One has to conform to certain conventions.

conscience	....	mental guide to right behaviour
		Let your conscience be your guide in the way to behave.
conscious	....	aware of
		I was fully conscious of his presence in the room.
consistency	....	degree of density, being of firm mind
		The liquid was of the consistency of custard. He was remarkable for his consistency of purpose in the face of all discouragement.
constituency	....	parliamentary or local government election area
		Our member has sat for this constituency for the last twenty years.
co-operation	....	agreement for joint benefits
		With your co-operation, we shall bring the year to a successful conclusion.
corporation	....	body governing a city or a very large company
		The Corporation of London is responsible for the City of London. The General Motors Corporation is one of the largest firms in the U.S.A.
core	....	centre
		Do not eat the core of the apple.
corps	....	body of military personnel
		The Air Training Corps exists for young men interested in the R.A.F.
corpse	....	dead body
		The corpse was taken to the mortuary.
credible	....	believable
		Baron Munchausen's stories are really not credible.
creditable	....	deserving praise
		Her examination results are most creditable.
critic	....	a judge of artistic, musical or literary work
		The critic wrote that he enjoyed the film.
critique	....	a critical essay
		A good critique gives both the best and the worst of a book.
cynical	....	fault-finding, not believing in human goodness
		The cynical man refused to believe in the other's generosity.
sceptical	....	given to questioning facts and conclusions
		I am sceptical about the success of the new plans.

deceased or diseased?

deceased	....	dead
		The deceased left his house at eight o'clock on the day he died.
diseased	....	affected by disease, unhealthy
		The surgeons amputated the diseased limb. Some people think modern art the product of diseased imaginations.
deference	....	respect
		Whatever we may think of a man personally, he should be treated with the deference due to his office.
difference	....	points which are unlike, disagreement, quantity by which amounts differ
		Even their mother could see no difference in the identical twins. The difference of opinion was not resolved by the board. There was a difference of £20 between the two estimates.
demur	....	to raise objections
		He carried out his duties without demur.
demure	....	composed, modest
		In the midst of all the uproar, her expression remained demure. Victorian maidens were expected to be demure.
depraved	....	corrupted
		The Rake's Progress tells the story of a depraved young man.
deprived	....	without some essential thing
		There are too many deprived people in the world.
deprecate	....	express disapproval of
		We can only deprecate the behaviour of our representative in refusing to send your complaints to us.
depreciate	....	lose in value
		Cars depreciate rapidly.
desert	....	barren land, leave
		Much of Arabia is desert. He deserted his wife.
dessert	....	fruit and nuts etc. at the end of a meal
		At dinner parties the ladies used to withdraw after the dessert.

desolate	....	barren, deserted, inconsolable
		The desert is desolate. The widow was desolate.
dissolute	....	without morals, lewd
		Many eighteenth century gentlemen were dissolute.
device	....	plan, emblem
		A device whereby pensions could be paid at 55 was worked out by the company. The house-flag carried a device in blue and gold.
devise	....	plan, assign
		We must devise a means of overcoming the problem. Wills devise property to heirs.
disburse	....	hand out
		Monasteries used to disburse alms.
disperse	....	scatter
		The crowd was made to disperse by the police.
discriminate	....	show differences between
		People who are colour-blind cannot discriminate between green and red.
incriminate	....	involve in a crime
		His letter seemed to incriminate him in the robbery.
distrait	....	absent-minded
		Professors are alleged to be distrait and dizzy blondes distraite.
distraught	....	driven mad
		Lady Macbeth was distraught with guilt.

eclectic or electric?

eclectic	....	not exclusive in opinion, taste etc.
		The books showed his eclectic taste in reading.
electric	....	adjective from 'electricity'
		Most town houses have electric light.
eclipse	....	surpass, overshadow, intercept
		His flashes of genius eclipse the more pedestrian efforts of his colleagues. An eclipse occurs when the Earth intercepts the sun's light to the moon.
ellipse	....	oval; leaving out words necessary to the sense of a sentence
		The Oval cricket ground is an ellipse. Very close friends often use ellipses in conversation.

edition	....	form in which books, newspapers etc. are published
		The new edition of *Encyclopaedia Britannica* is due soon. This is the sports edition of the paper.
addition	....	noun from 'to add'
		2 + 2 is an addition. In addition, we visited Paris.
effect	....	result, bring about
		The effect of his action was felt by everyone. We must effect greater efficiency in the office.
affect	....	pretend to feel, move
		Hypocrites affect sympathy. The sight of her tears affected me greatly.
effrontery	....	insolence
		He had the effrontery to suggest that he was the only person able to understand the problem.
affront	....	insult
		His rude behaviour was an affront to his colleagues.
elegy	....	poem for the dead or past time
		Gray wrote an elegy in a country churchyard.
eulogy	....	praise
		The chairman's speech was a eulogy of the workers.
elicit	....	draw out
		We must elicit all possible information from the inventor.
illicit	....	illegal
		Moonshine is distilled in illicit stills.
eligible	....	suitable
		Victorian mamas looked for eligible young men as husbands for their daughters.
illegible	....	so badly written as to be indecipherable
		Many doctors develop illegible handwriting.
elusive	....	difficult to find or remember
		He's never in his office, he's most elusive.
illusive	....	deceptive
		Mirages are illusive.
emigrant	....	a person who leaves one country to settle elsewhere
		In most countries emigrants must have a work permit before they land.

immigrant	....	a person who settles in a country not his native land
		The white races in America are descendants of immigrants.
eminent	....	outstanding
		Sir Frank Whittle was an eminent engineer.
imminent	....	about to happen
		In August 1939 war was imminent.
emollient	....	softening agent
		Lanolin is a skin emollient.
emolument	....	payment, salary or fees
		After years of training one expects a reasonable emolument.
empire	....	overseas territory controlled by a nation
		Britain is rapidly granting independence to her empire.
umpire	....	referee in certain sports
		The umpire tied the cricketers' pullovers round his waist.
endemic	....	normally present
		The common cold is endemic in Europe.
epidemic	....	abnormal outbreak of disease
		Six cases of smallpox in England constitute an epidemic.
ensure	....	make certain
		Please ensure that all letters are posted on the day they are written.
insure	....	cover by insurance
		It is wise to insure one's house and personal property.
entomology	....	study of insects
		Today students of entomology have discovered much about the social behaviour of insects.
etymology	....	study of the origin of words
		The Oxford Dictionary gives the etymology and the definition of words.
epithet	....	a fitting adjective
		'Nice' is too vague to be an epithet.
epitaph	....	praise of the dead, usually on a tombstone
		Not every epitaph is serious.

equable	....	calm and unruffled
		Her equable temperament admirably fitted her for the job of personal assistant.
equitable	....	fair and just
		The equitable distribution of bonus was based on a percentage of salary.
era	....	period of time
		The era of Napoleon ended with his exile.
error	....	mistake
		The letter was retyped because of a spelling error.
erotic	....	of love
		'X' certificates are given to erotic films.
erratic	....	in fits and starts, irregular in conduct etc.
		He can be brilliant but his work is most erratic.
exotic	....	of foreign origin
		She was wearing an exotic perfume.
esoteric	....	only for the initiated
		Freemasonry is an esoteric society. Much modern poetry is esoteric.
exoteric	....	commonplace
		It is an exoteric notion that Richard III murdered his nephews.
eraser	....	india rubber
		Good typists never use an eraser.
erasure	....	place where a rubbing out has occurred
		A correctly done erasure is invisible.
essay	....	composition
		In most exams one has to write an essay.
assay	....	test of precious metals for purity
		There are official offices to assay and stamp gold and silver.
exceed	....	do more than permitted; be greater than
		Do not exceed your duties. His ambitions exceed his abilities.
accede	....	agree to a request etc.; take up office
		The directors accede to your request. Deputy chairmen accede to the chair.
except	....	exclude
		All, except him, were at the meeting. They except the candidates for election from the meeting during voting.
accept	....	agree, receive
		I accept your plan. We often accept presents.

excess	....	too much
		An excess of words is called verbiage.
access	....	entry
		That door gives access to the corridor.
exercise	....	exertion of muscles, limbs etc.
		All animals require exercise.
exorcise	....	drive out, especially ghosts
		There is a special service to exorcise ghosts.
expansive	....	large, expanding, effusive
		The firm does an expansive trade with the States.
		Please be more expansive in your explanation.
		His expansive thanks were embarrassing.
expensive	....	costly
		Large, perfect diamonds are expensive.
explicit	....	clearly stated
		Instructions should be explicit to avoid confusion.
implicit	....	hinted at but not actually stated
		A baby places implicit trust in his mother.
extant	....	still existing
		The first edition of *The Times* is extant.
extent	....	area covered
		The full extent of the factory is 26 acres.
extinct	....	no longer in existence
		Prehistoric monsters are extinct.

facet or faucet?

facet	....	side, viewpoint
		Diamonds are facet cut. His speech gave one a new facet on the problem.
faucet	....	water-tap
		Gold plated bath faucets are expensive.
facility	....	aptitude
		The research worker had great facility for his task.
felicity	....	happiness
		True felicity is one of the greatest gifts to mankind.
farther	....	more distant
		New York is farther from San Francisco than from London.
further	....	more distant in time or space
		We must look further forward than next year.
		Nothing was further from my thoughts.

ferment	....	verb from fermentation, excite
		Yeast is used to ferment beer. The agitator fermented the crowd.
foment	....	apply warmth to; instigate
		The patient was advised to foment the septic spot. The trouble was fomented by a group of hot-heads.
fiscal	....	concerning finance
		The Chancellor's Budget statement outlines the fiscal policy of the Government.
physical	....	of the body
		Athletics demands physical exertion.
flagrant	....	open, usually insolently so
		Her persistent lateness was a flagrant breach of office rules.
fragrant	....	sweet-smelling
		Violets are fragrant.
funeral	....	burial ceremony
		The general had a military funeral.
funereal	....	like a funeral in atmosphere
		The dark offices were gloomy and funereal.

genius or genus?

genius	....	brilliant person
		Shakespeare was a dramatic genius.
genus	....	groups of animals or plants having characteristics common only to that group
		Man belongs to the genus *Homo sapiens*.

human or humane?

human	....	of the human race
		Speech is a human characteristic.
humane	....	kindly, considerate
		It is humane to kill animals suffering from incurable diseases.

humidity	....	dampness of the air
		The humidity of equatorial forests is greater than that of the Poles.
humility	....	meekness
		She felt great humility in the presence of the Archbishop.
hypercritical	....	over critical
		Even his best staff leave because he is hypercritical.
hypocritical	....	pretending to emotions etc.
		You are hypocritical if you do not practise what you preach.

identify or indemnify?

identify	....	recognise
		Identi-kits help witnesses to identify criminals.
indemnify	....	make good a loss
		Insurance companies indemnify policy holders in case of fire.
illimitable	....	cannot be limited
		The possibilities are illimitable.
inimitable	....	uncopiable
		Sir Winston Churchill's oratory was inimitable.
illiterate	....	unable to read or write
		All very young children are illiterate.
obliterate	....	wipe out
		The bombardment had obliterated the village.
illusion	....	a wrong idea
		He suffers under the illusion that he is Alexander the Great.
allusion	....	reference to
		During his speech he made allusion to the company's debt to the retiring chairman.
immoral	....	against morality, evil
		It is immoral to be cruel to each other.
amoral	....	lacking any moral sense
		Many criminals are amoral and do not understand the difference between right and wrong.
immunity	....	freed from fear of punishment, disease
		His laisser-passer gave him immunity from customs control. Vaccination gives immunity from many diseases.

impunity	....	without punishment
		His charm enables him to say outrageous things with impunity.
impeccable	....	perfectly groomed
		The turn-out of a Guardsman must be impeccable.
implacable	....	unyielding
		Martial law is implacable.
implicit	....	hinted at but not actually stated
		A baby places implicit trust in his mother.
explicit	....	clearly stated
		Instructions should be explicit to avoid confusion.
impotent	....	without power
		The fire brigade were impotent because there was no water supply.
impudent	....	cheeky, insolent
		The boy was impudent to the farmer when he was caught in the orchard.
inane	....	silly
		We had an inane conversation about the weather.
insane	....	mad
		He is quite insane when he loses his temper.
incinerate	....	burn up
		In the autumn, gardeners incinerate the leaves.
insinuate	....	hint at
		Blackmailers insinuate rather than state their threats.
incredible	....	unbelievable
		Fairy stories are incredible only to adults.
incredulous	....	unbelieving
		His story was received in incredulous silence.
indelible	....	cannot be erased
		The Coronation made an indelible impression on the spectators.
inedible	....	cannot or must not be eaten
		Over salty food is inedible. Deadly nightshade berries are inedible.
ineligible	....	unsuitable
		He is ineligible by virtue of his age.
intelligible	....	understandable
		He gave an intelligible report of the meeting.

ingenious	....	artful, skilful Juke boxes have ingenious mechanisms.
ingenuous	....	simple, naive The heroine of many Victorian novels was ingenuous.
insidious	....	sly, creeping His insults were never open but insidious.
invidious	....	unpleasant, often unjust, attacking The workmen resented the invidious remark that they slacked.
insulate	....	protect from damage Electric cables are well insulated because of the danger from fire.
isolate	....	cut off Patients with infectious diseases are isolated. The blizzard isolated many villages.

lath or lathe?

lath	....	thin strip of wood The ceiling lath supports the plaster.
lathe	....	machine for turning Machine parts, based on the wheel, are made on a lathe.
loath	....	unwilling He was loath to retire.
loathe	....	detest Some people loathe spiders.
loose	....	not fixed Loose covers can be removed for washing.
lose	....	cease to have, by negligence Do not lose the instructions.

momentary, monetary or momentous?

momentary	....	for a moment The pause was momentary.
momentous	....	of great importance The Coronation was a momentous occasion.
monetary	....	concerned with money The Treasury is responsible for the monetary policy of the country.

moral	....	right principled A moral man will not willingly break his principles.
morale	....	spirit In spite of the difficulties, the men had a high morale.
morning	....	before noon Most offices open at nine in the morning.
mourning	....	black clothes worn as sign of grief over a death Full mourning is now rarely worn, even by close relatives.
obliterate	....	wipe out The bombardment had obliterated the village.
illiterate	....	unable to read or write All very young children are illiterate.
ordinance	....	statute, law The ordinance was signed by the governor.
ordnance	....	guns, artillery Ordnance survey maps were originally produced for the Royal Artillery.

partition or petition?

partition	....	division A partition divided the large room into two small ones.
petition	....	request to an official body or an important person Over a thousand people signed the petition about the betting shop.
persecute	....	harass The Inquisition used to persecute protestants.
prosecute	....	take legal action against The Crown prosecutes in criminal actions.
personal	....	private, individual He is resigning for personal reasons.
personnel	....	group of workers in a factory, office etc. The personnel manager is responsible for the welfare of employees.

perspective	....	art of drawing solid objects on a flat surface
		Perspective was re-discovered in the Italian Renaissance.
prospectus	....	circular describing school, course, business etc.
		The company prospectus set out the balance sheet very clearly.
physical	....	of the body
		Athletics demands physical exertion.
fiscal	....	concerning finance
		The Chancellor's Budget statement outlines the fiscal policy of the Government.
plaintiff	....	person bringing a civil action in court
		The plaintiff claimed damages for the loss of his car.
plaintive	....	(adj.) wailing, mournful
		The woman nagged in a plaintive voice.
poignant	....	painfully sharp
		That tune always brings me poignant memories of happier days.
pungent	....	biting, sharp
		There was a pungent smell of burning wood in the air.
practicable	....	able to be performed
		All suggestions put in the box must be practicable.
practical	....	actual as opposed to theoretical
		He was sent on a course to gain both practical and theoretical experience of the new machine.
precede	....	go before
		A firm order must precede the carrying out of the job.
proceed	....	go forward, continue
		A firm order must be placed before we proceed with the job.
prescribe	....	lay down with authority
		We must prescribe the procedure for dealing with these matters in the future.
proscribe	....	banish, outlaw
		To proscribe a criminal was common practice in the Middle Ages.

prophecy	....	noun: ability to foretell the future
		His prophecy of last year has come true.
prophesy	....	verb: foretelling the future
		It is hard to prophesy the outcome of such action.
prescription	....	noun from prescribe
		There is only one prescription to remedy this.
proscription	....	noun from proscribe
		Proscription lists were opened in France in the French Revolution.
preposition	....	part of speech showing connexions
		He fell down the stairs. . . . 'down' is the preposition showing the connection between fell and stairs.
proposition	....	suggestion, plan
		His proposition was that we should have a meal after we had been to the theatre.
rankle	....	be bitter about
		His failure to thank me still rankles.
wrangle	....	argue bitterly
		The heirs wrangle over the will.
recent	....	not long ago
		In January, Christmas is recent.
resent	....	harbour ill-feeling about
		Mean-spirited people resent another's success.
respectfully	....	with deference
		One should treat one's elders respectfully.
respectively	....	in order
		Numbers 16 and 18 were painted green and cream respectively.
reverend	....	title of a cleric
		The new Vicar is the Reverend Mr Smith.
reverent	....	respectful, devout
		Reverent behaviour is expected in church.

salutary or solitary?

salutary	....	beneficial
		A little opposition is often salutary.
solitary	....	alone
		Hermits are solitary by choice.

salvage	....	recoverable waste, save a ship or its cargo from loss
		Waste paper and rags are valuable as salvage. Sea-going tugs often salvage ships in very bad weather.
selvedge	....	woven border of cloth
		The manufacturer's name was printed on the selvedge of the material.
sceptical	....	given to questioning facts and conclusions
		I am sceptical about the success of the new plan.
cynical	....	fault-finding, not believing in human goodness
		The cynical man refused to believe in the other's generosity.
sceptre	....	staff of office of a sovereign
		The sceptre of England lies in the Wakefield Tower.
spectre	....	ghost
		Anne Boleyn's spectre has been seen in Hampton Court Palace.
seize	....	grab
		I seize every opportunity of getting out into the country.
cease	....	bring to an end
		Please cease typing whilst I telephone.
solder	....	soft metal for joining other metals
		A plumber wipes the joint with solder.
soldier	....	enlisted man in an army
		The soldier sprang to attention when the general came in.
spacious	....	roomy
		Good proportions make even a small room look spacious.
specious	....	plausible
		The rogue always had a specious reason.
spurious	....	false
		It is a crime to issue spurious money.
stable	....	place for keeping horses; steady
		Many a stable is now a garage. Prices must remain stable.
staple	....	basic industry, food etc.
		The staple product of much of the Middle East is oil.

statue	....	representation in stone, metal etc. Almost every London square has a statute.
stature	....	height He had increased in stature since I had last seen him, two years ago.
statute	....	law The Royal Assent turns a Bill into a statute.
soot	....	black deposit caused by fire Chimneys must be swept to free them of soot.
suit	....	fitting, matching clothing Blue does not suit everyone. He ordered a new suit for his wedding.
suite	....	people in attendance; set of things belonging together The Royal suite accompanied the Queen on all her tours. The new dining suite has arrived.
surplice	....	gown worn by clergy, choirboys A surplice is made of fine white linen.
surplus	....	excess At sale time shops get rid of surplus stocks.
symmetry	....	harmony, balance The rose bud gave symmetry to the flower arrangement.
cemetery	....	burial ground There were many headstones in the old cemetery.

tenor or tenure?

tenor	....	male singing voice of higher range; purport Caruso was a famous tenor. I do not like the tenor of your remarks.
tenure	....	system of tenancy, holding office Under this tenure rent is paid yearly. During the Mayor's tenure of office he is the chief magistrate of the borough.
transient	....	passing This difficulty is only transient.
transit	....	being transported The goods are in transit; we shipped them last week.

urban or urbane?

urban	....	of a town
		Urban development must stop at the green belt.
urbane	....	elegant, well-bred
		His urbane manners always achieved the impossible.

venal or venial?

venal	....	willing to be bribed
		The Minister of Petroleum was a particularly venal official.
venial	....	a pardonable fault
		Some people would consider telling white lies to be a venial sin.
veracious	....	truthful
		The witness gave a veracious account of the accident.
voracious	....	greedy to excess
		Small boys often have voracious appetites.
veracity	....	truth
		Although extraordinary, his tale had an air of veracity.
voracity	....	greed
		A voracity for information possessed him.

wrangle or rankle?

wrangle	....	argue bitterly
		The heirs wrangle over the will.
rankle	....	to be bitter about
		His failure to thank me still rankles.

EXERCISES

1 In the following passages, the words in italics are wrongly used for others that resemble them closely. Replace them by the ones which should have been used. (Do not write out the passage.)
   (a) The *solder's era* was reported to the sergeant whose *resent* promotion made him unable to overlook a *fragrant* breach of discipline and even the *humidity* of the private could not soothe his wrath.

(b) His failure to *incriminate* between *voracity* and *allusion* caused him to *loose* his *alley* and so led to his downfall.

(c) The *inane physical* policy was a *transit* problem to be solved by the *genus* and not by a *venial* official.

(d) The *extinct* of world ownership of *bouillon* is a *casual* factor in *apprising* the *momentary* policy of nations.

(e) On *human* grounds, those who suffer from the changes in *urbane tenor* must be *identified*. Such generosity will also improve the *moral* of the citizens at this critical time.

(f) This *faucet* of the *collusion* of ideas between the two men *depraved* the board of the ability to *precede*. The chairman said that the whole argument robbed him of *breathe* and rendered him speechless.

2 In each of the following sentences the blank space may be filled by one of the words in brackets. State which is the right word in each sentence.

A 1 His autobiography made an (inedible, indelible) impression on us.
  2 Boswell had a (veracious, voracious) appetite for all Johnsoniana.
  3 The girl's apparent lack of sincerity makes one feel that she is (hypercritical, hypocritical).
  4 The pass will give you (access, excess) to the best seats in the theatre.
  5 There was a new (lath, lathe) in the workshop for turning.

B 1 If the plan is to succeed, then everyone must give their full (co-operation, corporation).
  2 The office junior must treat the supervisor (respectfully, respectively).
  3 The Sistine Chapel is (illimitable, inimitable).
  4 It is such a sensible suggestion that I am sure no-one can (demur, demure).
  5 The whole question of (emollients, emoluments) for senior staff is under review.

C 1 All firms will shortly (adapt, adept, adopt) a national system of training.
  2 Cats like fish and (loath, loathe) water.
  3 Scots and English (rankled, wrangled) for years over the border-line between the two countries.
  4 She always takes a walk early in the (morning, mourning).
  5 We thought the rain would never (cease, seize).

D 1 Ever since Man invented money it has been (deprecating, depreciating) in value.
  2 There are often tenterhook marks in the (salvage, selvedge) of cloth.
  3 May 24th used to be (umpire, empire) day.

4 (immunity, impunity) is granted to diplomatic and consular staffs.

5 There is no point in asking for (advice, advise) if you are not going to take it.

E 1 The Intelligence (core, corps, corpse) gathers information for the armed services.
2 The United Nations Charter outlaws religious (persecution, prosecution).
3 It was impossible to (elicit, illicit) anything else from the witness.
4 He showed great (facility, felicity) in handling his tools.
5 The arctic wastes are (desolate, dissolute).

3 Explain clearly, without using illustrative sentences, the difference in meaning between each of the following pairs:

A credible, creditable; obliterate, illiterate; plaintiff, plaintive; reverend, reverent; deceased, diseased.

B ferment, foment; accept, except; partition, petition; stature, statute; eraser, erasure.

C device, devise; poignant, pungent; critic, critique; ordinance, ordnance; epithet, epitaph.

D salutary, solitary; cloth, clothes; eclipse, ellipse; apposite, opposite; insulate, isolate.

E amoral, immoral; emigrant, immigrant; farther, further; desert, dessert; suit, soot.

F funereal, funeral; addition, edition; impeccable, implacable; confirm, conform; ensure, insure.

4 Show clearly that you understand the meaning of the following words by incorporating each of them in a separate sentence.

A accede; exceed; adverse; averse; affect; effect.
B calendar; calender; capital; capitol; consistency; constituency.
C deference; difference; allusion; illusion; ineligible; illegible.
D exercise; exorcise; impotent; impudent; sceptre; spectre.
E prophecy; prophesy; practical; practicable; elegy; eulogy.
F censer; censure; eminent; imminent; prescribe; proscribe.

5 Each of the following sentences contain mis-used words. Write down (i) the incorrect word and (ii) the word which should have been used. Do NOT copy the sentence out.

A 1 The house is all eclectic.
2 It is a pity that she effects such an accent.
3 She was distrait when she heard the news.
4 Counsels insinuate the rubbish.
5 His explanation was very clear and implicit.

B 1 I do not advice you to answer the letter.
2 That coat is far more expansive than the other.
3 There was no conscience effort in the athlete's style of running.
4 If you wish to be insidious, please say clearly what you mean.
5 The artist had difficulty with the prospectus of his drawings.

C 1 The room had a very specious look.
  2 His conceit led to his affront.
  3 There was sharp rise in the number of cases of measles, leading to an endemic.
  4 The porch spoilt the cemetery of the house.
  5 The ingenuous idea was so simple that we had none of us thought of it.
D 1 The doctor wrote out a prescription for his patient.
  2 You will be sorry if you seize your piano practice.
  3 The distinguished entomologist explained the derivation of the word.
  4 There was an incredible expression on her face as she listened to our explanation.
  5 In spite of the uneven floor the three-legged table was very staple.
E 1 The board has agreed to his preposition.
  2 The connoisseur showed an acetic taste in the collection of pictures.
  3 The crowd was asked to disburse quietly.
  4 Employees and their relatives are not illegible for this competition.
  5 Last year's trading figures show a very pleasing surplice.
F 1 The allusive word was on the tip of his tongue.
  2 He was very cynical about the prospects of our success.
  3 His biography gives a full account of his personal experiences.
  4 The thongs tying his wrists made his hands impudent.
  5 His temper is far too exotic to be called equitable.

6 In the following passage the words in italics are wrongly used for others which resemble them closely. Replace them by the ones which should have been used. (Do not write out the passage.)

As the explorers moved along the edge of a *precipitate* cliff with a *shear* drop below of hundreds of feet, a *hoard* of savages began to hurl their *missives* at them.

7 In each of the following sentences the blank space may be filled by one of two words. State which is the right word in each sentence. Do *not* copy the whole sentence:

  (i) I should not (advice, advise) you to do that.
  (ii) You must not (lose, loose) heart if you fail.
  (iii) The (decent, descent) of the mountain was dangerous.
  (iv) The first (addition, edition) of Shakespeare's plays is valuable.
  (v) The council was (composed, comprised) of men and women.

8 Explain clearly, without using illustrative sentences, the difference in meaning between the words in each of the following pairs:

ceremonial, ceremonious; patent, patient; impetus, impetuous; globular, cylindrical; antiquated, anticipated.

9 Show clearly that you understand the meaning of the following words by incorporating each of them in a separate sentence.

   (a) Effective
   (b) Efficient
   (c) Imaginary
   (d) Imaginative
   (e) Effect
   (f) Affect

10 Each of the following sentences contains a misused word. Write down (i) the incorrect word and (ii) the word which should have been used. Do *not* copy the sentence out.

   (i) I have to work on alternative Saturdays;
   (ii) He lives in a counsel house;
   (iii) Temperatures will be above the reasonable average;
   (iv) My uncle is the principle of the technical college;
   (v) He rejected my offer with a contemptible wave of the hand;
   (vi) John and Helen were born respectfully in London and Eastbourne.

6 dozen scarfs...
... or scarves?

5

Plurals

For all who would write and transcribe correct English, the plural forms are another set of 'trigger' words. We shall study them under two headings—Formation and Agreement.
Formation—The rule for making the plural of nouns in English is to add *s* to the singular form. However, some words retain the plural form of the older language (like *woman/women*), some words take the plurals of the foreign languages from which they have been borrowed (like *crisis/crises*), and in a third group are words having two plurals (like *penny—pence/pennies*) with different meanings or uses.
Agreement—Some nouns have a singular meaning with a plural form (like *news*) and therefore take a singular verb (e.g. What's the news = *What is the news?*); others have a plural meaning with a singular form (like *people*) and take a plural verb (e.g. *The people are worried*); and a third group of nouns are collective and they may be followed by a singular or plural verb according to the sense (e.g. *The Group is too large/A third group of nouns are collective and they may be followed by a singular or plural verb.*)

Formation of plurals

1 Most nouns add -*s* to the singular: *letter/letters*.

2 Nouns ending in *s, ss, ch, sh, x* and *z* add -*es*: *gas/gases, mass/masses, rich/riches, dish/dishes, tax/taxes, waltz/waltzes*.

3 (*a*) Nouns ending in consonant-y, change the *y* to *i* and add -*es*: *company/companies, lady/ladies, authority/authorities*.

(*b*) Nouns ending in vowel-y follow rule 1: *monkey/monkeys*.

4 There is no hard and fast rule for nouns ending in *f*. Here are the most common.

| knife | knives | handkerchief | handkerchiefs |
| thief | thieves | belief | beliefs |

half	halves	chief	chiefs
shelf	shelves	dwarf	dwarfs
wife	wives	hoof	hoofs
leaf	leaves	roof	roofs

scarf—scarfs or scarves
wharf—wharfs or wharves

5 There is no hard and fast rule for nouns ending in *o*. Here are the most common.

studio	studios	tomato	tomatoes
piano	pianos	potato	potatoes
solo	solos	cargo	cargoes
radio	radios	motto	mottoes

6 Foreign words retaining their original plural endings:

Latin:	stimulus	stimuli	Greek:	criterion	criteria
	terminus	termini		phenomenon	phenomena
	addendum	addenda		analysis	analyses
	datum	data		axis	axes
	agendum	agenda		crisis	crises
	erratum	errata		diagnosis	diagnoses
	bacterium	bacteria		thesis	theses
	stratum	strata		oasis	oases
French:	tableau	tableaux	Italian:	virtuoso	virtuosi
	bureau	bureaux		libretto	libretti
	Madame	Mesdames*		dilettante	dilettanti

7 The following nouns have two plurals, one native and one English. There is a tendency to use the anglicised form for the colloquial use, and the native plural for the scientific or specialised use.

formula	formulae	formulas
genius	genii (spirits)	geniuses (persons having unusual intellectual power)
syllabus	syllabi	syllabuses
memorandum	memoranda	memorandums
appendix	appendices	appendixes
index	indices (in mathematics)	indexes (in books)
bandit	banditti	bandits

The following English words also have two plural forms:

| brother | brothers | brethren |
| penny | pennies | pence |

* Also used as the plural of Mrs, or when preceding a list of women's names, e.g. Mesdames Hart, Leach and Corinth.

8 Some nouns form their plurals by adding -en or changing the internal vowels:

man	men*	goose	geese
woman	women*	tooth	teeth
child	children*	mouse	mice
ox	oxen*	foot	feet

9 Most compound nouns form their plurals by adding the plural ending to the most important word:

aide-de-camp	aides-de-camp
court-martial	courts-martial
son-in-law	sons-in-law
man-servant	men-servants
passer-by	passers-by
runner-up	runners-up
consul general	consuls general
major general	major generals
handful	handfuls
spoonful	spoonsful

10 Letters, numbers, and some words (when referred to as words) form their plurals by adding 's to the singular:

Dot your i's and cross your t's.
Three 7's are twenty-one.
Mind your p's and q's.
I don't like all these do's and don'ts.

Agreement

1 These nouns are plural in form but singular in meaning and therefore take a singular verb:

economics	measles
ethics	whereabouts
news	physics

e.g. Measles is an infectious disease.

2 Some nouns are singular in form but plural in meaning and therefore take a plural verb:

people   congregation   audience   clientèle

e.g. The congregation were asked to pay their magazine subscriptions before the end of the month.

* Remember that this group of words forms an important exception to the rule for forming the possessive, see page 13. The possessive forms are *men's, women's, children's, oxen's*.

3 Some nouns may be used as either singular or plural according to their meaning within the context of the sentence.

> committee   acoustics
> jury   association
> company   number

e.g. The committee has agreed upon the course to be taken. The committee have disagreed on several points.

EXERCISES

1. Write down the plural form of the following words; then write a sentence using each of the words.
   (a) wolf, serf, cuff, calico, domino, embargo, halo, innuendo, tornado, veto.
   (b) life, alto, banjo, concerto, contralto, piccolo, albino, cameo, casino, curio.
   (c) Eskimo, kimono, ratio, memento, tomato, dynamo, echo, man-of-war, cupful, Miss.
   (d) Mr, 1950, apparatus, diagnosis, fungus, maximum, libretto, synopsis, scenario, postmaster-general.

2. Write sentences showing the difference in meaning or usage for both plural forms of the following words:

   genius, penny, brother, index, bandit

3. Use the following words in sentences, taking care not to commit errors of agreement:

   ethics, whereabouts, economics, audience, people, clientèle, jury, committee, number, staff, company, athletics, crew, trousers, scissors, statistics, nuptials, annals, politics, series.

4. Write the plural form of each of the following words:

   dairy, half, echo, potato, radius, journey, roof, basis, appendix, son-in-law.

5. Give the plurals of the following words:

   chimney; son-in-law; passer-by; me; piano; oasis; ass; his; potato; memory.

6. Rewrite the following sentences in the plural:
   (i) The chief kept his wife's piano on the roof.
   (ii) The witch changed the man and the baby into a donkey and a deer.
   (iii) This artist's canvas looks as if he painted it with his foot.
   (iv) The dormouse in the box is hers, not mine.

7 Rewrite these sentences in the plural wherever possible:
   (i) The valley is not shown in this atlas.
   (ii) I read a child's story in that woman's magazine.
   (iii) My godson was told to take a spoonful of his doctor's medicine.
   (iv) I am going to have my frock cleaned next week.

English Reference Books

The Dictionary. Most people regard the dictionary primarily as a guide to correct spelling. It is unfortunate and surprising that the dictionary has acquired this reputation because it tells us so much more about words than how to spell them; and as a guide to spelling it does not always give us the help we are seeking.

Some of the commonest spelling errors occur through doubts about double consonants, e.g. *travel—traveling* or *travelling*? and doubts about mute *e*'s, e.g. *issue—issueing* or *issuing*? Most dictionaries do not include these verb forms, which means that other sources (mentioned later in this chapter) must be consulted to settle these queries.

Arrangement. To derive the greatest benefit from your dictionary, you must first of all learn how to use it. The words in a dictionary are, of course, arranged alphabetically, but in some dictionaries only the root (or key) words are arranged alphabetically. Consider the two extracts opposite.

You will see that in the Oxford Dictionary the words 'careful' and 'careless' are listed in their alphabetical position after 'career' and before 'caress', where in Chambers's Dictionary they are treated as derivatives of the root word 'care' and appear in the same paragraph. The system of word arrangement will be explained in the Introduction to your dictionary. Study this carefully so that you will always be able to find the word you are seeking as quickly as possible.

cāre¹, *n.* Solicitude, anxiety; occasion for these; serious attention, heed, caution, pains, (*take, have a,* ~, be cautious); charge, protection, (*A, c/o* or ~ *of B,* in addresses; *have the, take,* ~ *of; in, under,* one's ~); thing to be done or seen to (~*s of State* etc.; *that shall be my* ~); ~-*laden,* -*worn,* with anxieties; ~' *taker,* person hired to take charge, esp. of house in owner's absence, (adj.) exercising temporary control, as *a* ~*taker* (stopgap) *government.* [OE *caru,* OS *cara,* OHG *chara,* ON *kör,* Goth. *kara* f. Gmc •*karō*]

cāre², v.i. Feel concern or interest *for* or *about;* provide food, attendance, etc., *for* (children, invalids, etc.); (w. neg. expressed or implied) feel regard, deference, affection, *for,* be concerned *whether* etc., (often with expletive *a pin, a damn, a farthing, a tinker's cuss; couldn't* ~ *less,* colloq., be utterly indifferent; *I don't* ~ *if I do,* am willing); be willing or wishful *to* (*should not* ~ *to be seen with him; do you* ~ *to try them?*). [OE *carian* f. Gmc]• *karō-jan* (prec.)]

careen', *v.t. & i.* Turn (ship) on one side for cleaning, caulking, etc.; (cause to) heel over; •(of vehicle etc.) career wildly. [ult. f. L *carina* keel]

careen'age, *n.* Careening a ship; expense of it; place for it. [f. prec. + -AGE]

career', *n. & v.t.* **1.** Swift course, impetus, (*in full, mid,* etc., ~); course or progress through life; development & success of party, principle, nation, etc.; way of making a livelihood (*a* ~ *diplomat,* a professional); hence ~IST (3) *n.,* one intent mainly on personal advancement & success in life. **2.** *v.i.* Go swiftly or wildly (often *about*). [f. F *carrière* f. It. -*icra* f. Rom. •*carraria* (*via*) carriage- (road) f. L *carrus* CAR¹]

care'ful (-ärf-), *a.* Concerned *for,* taking care *of;* painstaking, watchful, cautious, (*to do, that, what, whether,* etc.); done with or showing care. Hence ~LY² *adv.,* ~NESS *n.* [OE *carful;* see -FUL]

care'less (-ārl-), *a.* Unconcerned, lighthearted; inattentive, negligent (*of*), thoughtless; inaccurate. Hence

The Concise Oxford Dictionary

care, *kār, n.* affliction: anxiety: heedfulness: charge, keeping: the cause or object of anxiety.—*v.i.* to be anxious (for, about): to be disposed, willing (to): to have a liking or fondness (for): to provide (for). *adjs.* care'-free', light-hearted; care'ful, full of care: heedful: (*B.*) anxious.—*adv.* care'fully.—*n.* care'fulness.—*adj.* care'less, without care: heedless, unconcerned.—*adv.* care'lessly.—*ns.* care'lessness; care'tak'er, one put in charge of anything, esp. a building.—*adj.* care'worn, worn or vexed with care.—take care, to be cautious; take care of, to look after with care. [O.E. *caru;* O.N. *kaera,* to lament.]

careen, *ka-rēn', v.t.* to lay a ship on her side to repair her bottom and keel.—*v.i.* to heel over. [Fr. *carène*—L. *carina,* the bottom of a ship, the keel.]

career, *ka-rēr', n.* a race: a rush: progress through life, esp. advancement in calling or profession.—*v.i.* to move or run rapidly. [Fr. *carrière,* a racecourse.]

caress, *kā-res', v.t.* to touch endearingly, to fondle.—*n.* an endearing touch. [Fr. *caresser*—It. *carezza,* an endearment; Low L. *cāritia—cārus,* dear.]

caret, *kar'ét, n.* a mark, , to show where to insert something omitted. [L., 'there is wanting.']

cargo, *kär'gō, n.* the goods a ship carries: its load:—*pl.* car'goes. [Sp. from root of car.]

Carib, *kar'ib, n.* one of a native race inhabiting parts of Central America and the north of South America, or their language.—*adj.* Caribbē'an. [From Sp.; cf. cannibal.]

caribou, *kar-i-bōō', n.* the American reindeer. [Canadian Fr.]

caricature, *kar'i-kä-tyùr, n.* a likeness or imitation so exaggerated or distorted as to appear ridiculous.—*v.t.* to make ridiculous by an absurd likeness or imitation.—*n.* caricatur'-ist. [It. *caricatura—caricare,* to load, from root of car.]

caries, *kā'ri-ēz, n.* decay, esp. of teeth.—*adj.* cārious, decayed. [L.]

Chambers's Shorter English Dictionary

Pronunciation. Most dictionaries indicate how words should be pronounced. Some dictionaries do this by using phonetic symbols; others repeat in brackets any syllables that may cause doubts. You will find an explanation of the various signs and symbols in the Introduction to the dictionary.

> crētā′ceous (-sh*us*), a. Of (the nature of) chalk: (~ *system* (Geol.), third and final system of the Mesozoic group of rocks. [f. L *cretaceous* (*creta* chalk, see -ACEOUS)]

The Concise Oxford Dictionary

The stress mark (′) tells you which syllable of the word is accented, that is, spoken a little more forcefully than the other syllables. The accent falls on the syllable before the stress mark. The *diacritical marks* (ĕ, ā, ă) tell you how to pronounce the vowels.

Parts of speech. The *a.* following *cretaceous* indicates that the word is an adjective.

Meaning. The main part of each entry tells the meaning of the word. With homonyms such as *bar* each meaning is defined and numbered.

> bar¹, n. 1. Long piece of rigid material (metal, wood, soap, etc.; ~-*bell*, iron ~ with ball at each end used in gymnastics, cf. *dumb-bell*; ~′*wood*, red wood from Gaboon imported in ~s for dyeing etc.). 2. Slip of silver below clasp of medal as additional distinction; band of colour etc. on surface, (Her.) two horizontal parallel lines across shield (~ *sinister*, by mistake for BEND or BATON, supposed sign of illegitimacy). 3. Rod or pole used to confine or obstruct (*window, door, grate, gate, -*~); barrier of any shape (*Temple Bar, toll*′~); sandbank or shoal at mouth of harbour or estuary. 4. (Mus.) vertical line across stave dividing piece into sections of equal time-value, such sections; immaterial barrier; (Law) plea arresting action or claim; moral obstacle. 5. Barrier with some technical significance, as, in lawcourt, place at which prisoner stands; hence ~ *of conscience, opinion*, etc.; ‖*trial at* ~, in Queen's Bench division; a particular court (*practise at parliamentary, Chancery*, etc., ~); ‖ *be called to the* ~ (i.e. that in Inns of Court separating benches), be admitted a barrister; ‖ *be called within the* ~ (i.e. that in courts within which Q.C.s plead), be appointed Queen's Counsel; *the* ~, barristers, profession of barrister. 6. ‖(Parl.) rail dividing off space to which non-members may be admitted on business. 7. (In an inn etc.) counter across which refreshments are handed, space behind or room containing it; ‖~′*man,* ~′*maid,* •~-*tender,* attendants at such counter. [ME & OF *barre* f. LL *barra* etym. dub.]

Derivation. At the end of each entry you will find an explanation of the origin of the word. This tells you from which language a word comes and what it originally meant in that language. In this entry F means French. A list of dictionary abbreviations will be given in the Introduction.

> **gobe′mouche** (gob′mōōsh), n. (pl. ~s pr. like sing.). Credulous newsmonger. [f. F *gobe-mouches* lit. fly-catches (*gober* swallow, *mouches* flies)]

Plural forms. The dictionary indicates plural forms which may cause doubt.

> **sīl′o**, n. (pl. ~s), & v.t. 1. Pit or airtight structure in which green crops are pressed & kept for fodder undergoing fermentation. 2. v.t. Make ensilage of. [Sp. f. L f. Gk *siros*]

Use of capitals. The dictionary will sometimes help you with capitalisation queries, e.g. should you use an initial capital in Australian?

> **Austrāl′ian**, n. & a. Native of, resident in, Australia; (adj.) of Australia. [f. F *Australien* f. L as AUSTRAL]

Special information. Most dictionaries include information about famous persons and places.

> **Ju′piter** (jōō-), n. (Rom. myth.) king of gods; ~ *Plu′vius* (plōō-) god of rain (joc.); largest planet of solar system. [L]

Usage. The dictionary tells you whether words are colloquial, slang, archaic or vulgar.

> **sca′ramouch**, n. (arch.). Boastful poltroon, braggart. [17th c., f. It. *Scaramuccia* stock character in Italian farce (=SKIRMISH); pres. sp. f. F -*mouche*]

> **chipp′y̆**, a. (sl.). Dry, uninteresting; parched & queasy after drunkenness etc.; irritable. Hence ~-INESS n. [CHIP¹ + -Y²]
> **Chips**, n. (naut. sl.). Ship's carpenter. [pl. of CHIP¹, cf. BUTTONS]

> ‖**snaf′fle²**, v.t. (sl.). Appropriate, purloin, pinch. [c. 1700, cant of unkn. orig.]
> •**snafu′** (-fōō), a. & n. (Service sl.). 1. Chaotic. 2. n. Utter confusion. [f. initial letters of 'situation *n*ormal, *a*ll *f*ouled *u*p'.]

> **slipp′y**, a. Slippery (colloq.); *look* or *be* ~ (sl.), look sharp, make haste. [-Y²]

Idioms. Idiomatic expressions and idioms are listed under key words. What is the meaning of 'to take silk'?

> silk, n. 1. Fine soft thread produced in making cocoon by ~'-*worm* or larva of kinds of moth feeding esp. on mulberry leaves (*spun* ~, see SPIN; *thrown* ~, ORGANZINE): similar thread spun by some spiders etc. or (*artificial* ~, now usu. *rayon*) thread or yarn made from cellulose. 2. Cloth woven of ~ (‖*take* ~, become K.C. or Q.C. & exchange stuff for ~ gown); (pl.) kinds, or garments made, of such cloth. 3. ‖ (colloq.). K.C. or Q.C. 4. Peculiar lustre seen in some sapphires & rubies. 5. (attrib., now usu. preferred to *silken*). Made of ~ (~ *stockings* etc.; *make a ~ purse out of a sow's ear*, get better results from a person than his qualities admit of). 6. ‖ ~-*fowl*, breed with silky plumage . . .

Abbreviations. General abbreviations are listed in an Appendix to the *Concise Oxford Dictionary.*

There are three other appendices on Pronunciation of Non-English words, Pronunciation of Proper Names, and Weights and Measures.

Pitman's English/Shorthand Dictionary, although primarily a reference book for Pitman shorthand writers, is used by many typists as a spelling guide even though they may be transcribing from audio-dictation or other shorthand systems. The book is a combined shorthand and English dictionary; with each word is listed its shorthand outline. As each word has a different shorthand outline, the derivatives as well as the root words are listed in alphabetical order. For example, if you cannot remember whether the word 'benefited' has one or two t's, an ordinary dictionary gives no assistance. In a shorthand dictionary, however, 'benefited' is listed after 'benefit' because the shorthand outline is different.

Good English by G. H. Vallins. As the author writes in the first chapter, 'Scope and Aims of this Book', 'In some respects it is, in fact, a utility reference book. The unpractised writer who sucks his pen hopefully over the still virgin paper will, it is hoped, find something of value in its pages.' *Good English* deals with sentence patterns, spelling, punctuation, idiom, letter writing and usage; it will help you to become sensitive to good English by giving examples of bad English—bad, that is, in the sense that, for one reason or another, it does not exactly express the meaning intended. The book also contains collections of sentences taken from newspapers and journals, for criticism. At the end of the book are the author's 'answers' with which you can compare your own comments.

Modern English Usage, by H. W. Fowler, is generally accepted to be the standard work of reference on English usage. By 'usage' we mean the customary practice of the best writers and speakers. Whenever you are not sure which of two words to use (e.g. 'dreamt' or 'dreamed') or when you cannot remember some point of grammar (such as whether 'each of them is' or 'each of them are' is correct) refer to Fowler's *M.E.U.* and you will usually find a ruling on the question.

Roget's Thesaurus of English Words and Phrases arranges words in groups according to their meaning, and association of ideas. Where it is meaningful a section of words will have their opposites or near opposites printed in an adjoining column. To use the book you must first look up the word in question in the index. The number against the word refers you to the section in which the word occurs. In that section you will find all the other words and phrases used in English which have a similar meaning, or which follow each other by association of ideas.

> 694. **Director**—N. director, manager, governor, rector, comptroller; superintendent, -visor; intendant; over-seer, -looker; foreman, boss; super-cargo, inspector, visitor, ranger, surveyor, moderator, monitor, task-master; master &c. 745; leader, ring-leader, demagogue, conductor, fugleman, precentor, bell-wether, agitator.
>
> guiding star &c. 693; adviser &c. 695; guide &c. 527; pilot; helmsman; steersman; man at the wheel; wire-puller.
>
> driver, whip, Jehu, charioteer; coach-, cab-man, jarvey; postilion, muleteer, teamster; whipper in; engineer, engine driver, motorman, chauffeur.
>
> head, -man; principal, president, speaker; chairman; captain &c. 745; superior; dean; mayor &c. 745; vice-president, prime minister, premier, vizier, grand vizier; dictator.
>
> officer, functionary, minister, official, bureaucrat; Jack in office; office-bearer; person in authority &c. 745.
>
> statesman, strategist, legislator, lawgiver, politician, administrator, statist; arbiter &c. 967; king maker, power behind the throne.
>
> board &c. 696.
>
> secretary, -of state; vicar &c. 759; steward, factor; agent &c. 758; bailiff, middleman; ganger, clerk of works; factotum, major-domo, seneschal, housekeeper, shepherd, croupier, proctor, procurator, curator, librarian.
>
> Adv. ex officio.
>
> •
>
> 695. **Advice**—N. advice, counsel, adhortation; word to the wise; suggestion, submonition, recommendation, advocacy, consultation.
>
> exhortation &c. 615; expostulation &c. 616; admonition &c. 668; guidance &c. 693.
>
> instruction, charge, injunction.
>
> adviser, prompter; counsel, -lor; monitor, mentor, Nestor, senator; teacher &c. 540.
>
> guide, manual, chart &c. 527.
>
> physician, leech; arbiter &c. 967.
>
> reference; consultation, conference, parley &c. 696.
>
> V. advise, counsel; give -advice, -counsel, -a piece of advice; suggest, prompt, recommend, prescribe, advocate; exhort &c. 615.
>
> enjoin, enforce, charge, instruct, call; call upon &c. 765; dictate.
>
> expostulate &c. 616; admonish &c. 668.
>
> advise with; lay heads-, consult- together; compare notes; hold a council, deliberate, be closeted with.

An extract from ROGET's THESAURUS

Usage and Abusage is one of many books written by Eric Partridge. The ground covered is similar to Fowler's *M.E.U.* but the subjects are treated from a different angle. The author has a pleasantly light and amusing style of writing and you will enjoy dipping into his books if the study of words and usage has begun to interest you.

The Complete Plain Words, by Sir Ernest Gowers, is a reconstruction of two previous books by the same author, *PlainWords* and *ABC of Plain Words*. Both these were written at the invitation of the Treasury as a contribution to what they were doing to improve official English. *The Complete Plain Words* is intended as a reference book for those who use words as tools of their trade in administration or business, and is concerned with the choice and arrangements of words in such a way as to get an idea as exactly as possible out of one mind into another. Simple, short communications enable all of us to complete our work more quickly. *The Complete Plain Words* will help you to write correctly and concisely, and to avoid using jargon, superfluous words and meaningless expressions, behind which some people hide their ignorance and muddled thinking.

EXERCISES

1 Refer to *Deskbook of Correct English* for the following information:
   (a) hyphenation (or non-hyphenation) of *coal hole, coal mine, coal man*
   (b) the difference between *premisses* and *premises*
   (c) a spelling rule for adding *ing* to words ending in *ic* such as *picnic*
   (d) a criticism of the expression 'my personal opinion is . . .'
   (e) hyphenation (or non-hyphenation) of *free will, freehold, free lance*
   (f) correct usage of the word *aggravate*
   (g) *per cent* or *per cent.*—which is correct?
   (h) hyphenation (or non-hyphenation) of *red herring, red hot, red currant*

2 Refer to *The Complete Plain Words* for simple words which can replace the following overworked official words:
   (a) inform
   (b) residence
   (c) transmit
   (d) initiate
   (e) commence
   and for information on the following:
   (f) difference between *compare to* and *compare with*
   (g) *the first two* or *the two first*—which is correct?

(h) usage of *less* and *fewer*
(i) difference between *forgo* and *forego*
(j) the use of *teenager* in place of *adolescent, juvenile* or *young person*

3 Find out the following information from your dictionary:
(a) the meaning of *muliebrity*
(b) the plural of *retina*
(c) the meaning of *D.P.H.*
(d) the meaning and anglicised pronunciation of *ensemble*
(e) the pronunciation of *Sioux*
(f) the derivation of *dividend*
(g) the meaning of *Rosicrucian*
(h) the meaning and derivation of *amanuensis*
(i) the plural of *crisis*
(j) the meaning of *cut off one's nose to spite one's face*

4 Refer to *Usage and Abusage* for the following information:
(a) nouns of assemblage for: *sausages, boys, tourists, cats*
(b) the difference between *everyone* and *every one*
(c) the difference between *Great Britain* and *The United Kingdom*
(d) comment on *gipsy/gypsy*
(e) comment on *anent*
(f) comment on *ketchup/catchup/catsup*
(g) what is understood by *Johnsonese*
(h) the difference between *biannual* and *biennial*
(i) an example of a battered simile
(j) *Welsh rabbit* or *Welsh rarebit*—which is correct?

5 Explain the following dictionary entries:

(a) indĕl'ible a. (Of mark, stain, ink, etc., & fig. of disgrace etc.) that cannot be blotted out. Hence ~IBIL'ITY n., ~ibly adv. (f. L. IN*delebilis* f. *delere* blot out.)

(b) escŭtch'eon (-chon), n. Shield with armorial bearings; *a blot on his* ~ (stain on reputation); middle of ship's stern where name is placed; pivoted key-hole cover. (f. ONF *esuchon* f. LL *scutionem*, L. *scutum* shield.)

(c) dāt'um, n. (pl. *-ta*). Thing known or granted, assumption or premiss from which inferences may be drawn; fixed starting-point of scale etc. (ORDNANCE ~). (L, neut. p.p. of *dare* give.)

6 To which reference books would you refer in the following circumstances?
(a) You have a letter from a Mr Urquhart and wish to speak to him on the telephone, but you are not sure how to pronounce his name.
(b) You are employed by a wholesale firm of men's outfitters. You receive an order from America for 3 gross men's vests, colour dark grey. Your firm manufactures only white vests and as dark grey is an unusual colour for vests, it occurs to you that perhaps the word *vest* has a different meaning in America.
(c) You are transcribing the sentence 'Over seven hundred and eighty-six employees have had between five and ten years'

experience in a comparable industry.' You wish to refer to some rules for writing numbers in figures or words.

(d) You are transcribing the words *sand bag* and want to know whether to hyphenate them or write them as one word or two words.

7 Explain the following dictionary entries:

(a) sill'y, a. & n. 1. ‖ Innocent, simple, helpless, (arch.); foolish weak-minded, imprudent, unwise, imbecile; ‖ *the ~y season,* August & September as the season when newspapers start trivial discussions for lack of news; *~y point, short leg* (placed close up to batsman). 2. n. (colloq.). A ~y person. Hence ~ILY² adv., ~INESS n. [later form of ME *sely* (dial. *seely*) f. OE *saelig, OS, OHG *sālig,* f. WG *sæli* luck, happiness]

(b) crème (-ām), n. ~ *de menthe* (dəmahnt), peppermint liqueur ~ *de la* ~ (-dlah-), the very pick, élite. [F]

(c) scāpe'goat (-pg-), n. (O.T.) goat allowed to escape when Jewish chief priest had laid sins of people upon it (*Lev.* xvi); person bearing blame due to others. [SCAPE¹]

(d) jŭnk¹, n. & v.t. Old cable cut up for oakum etc.; discarded material, rubbish; lump, chunk; (naut.) salt meat; lump of tissue in sperm-whale, containing spermaceti; ~-*shop,* marine store, (derog.) antique dealer's shop; (v.t.) divide into ~s. [f. 1485, of unkn. orig.] jŭnk², n. Flat-bottomed sailing vessel used in Chinese seas. [16th c., app ult. f. Javanese *djong*]

(e) harb'inger (-j-), n. & v.y. One who announces another's approach, forerunner (formerly) one sent to purvey lodgings for army, royal train, etc.; (v.t.) announce approach of. [ME, f. OF *herbergere* f. *herberge* lodging f. WG *heriberga*

(her army + *bergan* protect); -n- as in *messenger*]

(f) ŏc'topus, n. (pl. ~es). (Kinds of) cephalopod mollusc with eight suckered arms round mouth; organized & usu. harmful ramified power or influence. [f. Gk *oktopous* eight-footed (OCTO-, *pous* foot)]

(g) hăn'som(căb), n. Two-wheeled cabriolet for two inside, with driver mounted behind and reins going over roof. [*Hansom* patentee, 1834]

(h) slĭth'er (-dh-), v.i. (colloq.). Slide unsteadily, go with irregular slipping motion. [ME var. of (now dial.) *slidder* (cf. *hither*) f. OE *slid(e)rian* frequent. f. *slid,* weak grade of *slid-* SLIDE]

(i) crē'osōte, n. Colourless oily fluid distilled from wood-tar, a strong antiseptic; (Commerc.) carbolic acid. Hence crēs'OL n., caustic liquid obtained by distillation of coal tar. [f. Gk *kreas* meat + *sōzō* save]

(j) justice, n. Just conduct; fairness, exercise of authority in maintenance of right; *poetic(al)* ~, reward of virtue & punishment of vice; judicial proceedings, as *Court of J* ~; magistrate; judge, esp. (in England) of Supreme Court of Judicature, whence ~SHIP n.; *J~ of the Peace,* lay magistrate appointed to preserve peace in country, town, etc.; *do* ~ *to,* treat fairly, show due appreciation of; *do* one*self* ~, perform worthily of one's abilities. [ME, f. OF (*-ice, -ise*), f. L *justitia* (as

8 (a) A dictionary has the following:

Reign (rān). 1. n. Sovereignty, rule (under, in the r. of; the last three rr.).
2. v.i. be a sovereign; prevail or obtain (Silence reigns). (L. *rego,* rule.)

Explain: (rān); n.; rr.; v.i.; (L. *rego,* rule).

129

(b) Briefly and in the same manner write dictionary definitions of: onion; cook; bowl.

9. Give the meanings of the following:
   (a) c.i.f., e.g., i.e., N.B., E. & O.E., pro tem.
   (b) inter alia, bona fide, prima facie, ipso facto.

10. Write what you would expect to find in a small dictionary (e.g. the *Pocket Oxford Dictionary*) under the words:
    conduct; machinery; reaction

11. Write in full the following dictionary abbreviations:
    adj., dial., exc., fem., fig., fut., inf., int., prov., v. aux.

… havrriot memoranoq.

7
Composing Simple Communications

Shorthand-typists and audio-typists, in addition to their normal transcription work, are sometimes asked to compose simple communications from brief verbal instructions. These can be grouped under four headings:

1 *Internal memoranda*
'Just drop a note to Mr Robinson in our Plymouth office and confirm the meeting on Thursday, would you, please Brenda? Remind him that it's at Head Office this time and not at the factory as usual.'

2 *Transmittal letters*
'Would you send this form off to Mrs Swanson, please Nadia? Tell her to complete it and return it as soon as possible.'

3 *Letters of confirmation*
'Type a short letter to the hotel in Bridlington, please Gillian, to confirm the booking I made by 'phone this morning—a single room with bath for two nights, next Wednesday and Thursday. I'd like to sign the letter before I go to lunch, so will you do it at once, please?'

4 *Acknowledgments*
'The parcel of account books, vouchers, bank statements and so on arrived back from the auditors this morning, Leslie. Just drop them a written acknowledgment, will you please?'

Here are a few hints about composing from short verbal instructions which will help you to carry out those four instructions and others like them:

1 Collect all the information you require e.g. full name and initials of addressee, full address, dates, reference or order numbers.

2 Decide how you will display the communication e.g. in the form of a memorandum or as a letter.
3 Draft the content in longhand. Sometimes you can say all you need to say in a single sentence. Sometimes you will need two or three sentences. When in doubt, choose shorter rather than longer sentences. Start a new paragraph each time you introduce another topic. The following plan may be of help:

1st sentence or paragraph
State message as simply and directly as possible.

2nd sentence or paragraph
Give any additional information, if needed.

3rd (or last) sentence or paragraph
Suggest future action, if appropriate.

4 Decide how to close the letter. Who will sign it? What is the correct complimentary close?
5 When you have drafted the letter, read it through to make sure that it is:

Complete
Does it contain everything you were told to say?

Clear
Have you conveyed the message clearly so that there is no possibility of misunderstanding?

Courteous
Is the wording polite and is the tone appropriate? Are the salutation and complimentary close appropriate?

Dear Sir	Yours faithfully
Dear Sirs	
Dear Mr Brown	Yours sincerely

Correct
  (a) As regards all the numbers, figures, dates, amounts, sums of money, facts and details?
  (b) As regards spelling, punctuation, names, initials, wording? Use simple, everyday language; it is not necessary—indeed it is stuffy and old-fashioned to use jargon like *I am in receipt of your letter of 24th instant.* Simply write *Thank you for your letter of 24 May.*

Concise
Is the message short and to the point? Writing longer letters than are necessary wastes everybody's time.

6 When you are satisfied with the draft, decide on the paper you will use and the number of carbon copies needed. Feed the carbon pack into the machine and type the communication.
7 Before removing the work from the machine, read it through, check it and correct any errors.
8 Sign the letter or present it for signature.
9 Type an envelope if needed. Remember to select an envelope of the correct size and weight for the size of the letter and any enclosures.
10 Check enclosures and special mailing notations, such as *AIRMAIL, PERSONAL* or *REGISTERED POST*.
11 Despatch the letter as soon as possible after it has been signed, sealed and stamped or franked.

Remember that the letters you send out convey an image of your office to the people who receive them—and not only an image of your office but also of the whole organisation and the goods or services marketed by it. Furthermore, the ability to write a good letter is highly valued in the business world and if you prove to your employer that you can produce perfectly composed and typed communications without supervision, you will probably find yourself being considered for promotion to a more senior post.

Now we will consider the examples given at the beginning of the chapter and follow through the composition of the four communications, according to the list of hints given on page 131.

1 Internal memoranda
Some firms provide pre-printed forms for internal communications; in others the typist displays the information on a sheet of plain paper. In both cases the individual parts of the communication are the same:

(a) *Title*
INTEROFFICE MEMORANDUM
or
MEMORANDUM
or
INTERNAL MEMORANDUM

(b) *Heading which states:*

TO (name of addressee or addressees, in the case of multiple memoranda)
FROM (name and/or position of originator)
DATE
SUBJECT

REFERENCE (sometimes the reference is not included in the heading, in which case it can be typed at the left-hand lower edge of the page, against the margin).

These five items can be arranged in various ways as shown in the illustration below.

3 *The message*

4 The initials of the originator. Internal communications are usually initialled, not signed, but this is a matter of custom rather than a hard and fast rule.

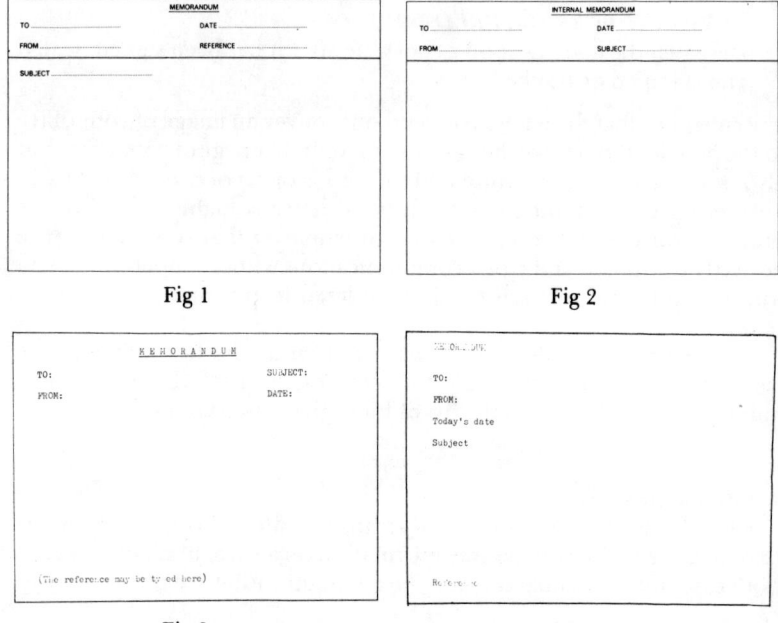

Fig 1

Fig 2

Fig 3

Fig 4

Examples of internal communications.

Figs 1 and 2 are pre-printed forms. The form shown in Fig 2 has no space for the reference in the heading, so the reference would be typed in the lower left-hand corner in line with the margin.

Figs 3 and 4 are examples of memoranda displayed on plain paper. Fig 4 is displayed in the fully-blocked style, i.e. each line starts at the left-hand margin.

Instruction

'Just drop a note to Mr Robinson in our Plymouth office and confirm the meeting on Thursday, would you, please Brenda? Remind him that it's at Head Office this time and not at the factory as usual.' (The Regional Marketing Director is speaking).

Working steps
1. Make sure you know Mr Robinson's initials and designation; look them up if necessary. If interoffice mail is pouched, i.e. each day's correspondence from all departments sent together in one large envelope, then a detailed address is not necessary. Check the date of the following Thursday, and time of meeting.
2. Let us assume that written communications between your office and the Plymouth office are in the form of internal memos and that your firm provides pre-printed forms.
3. Draft message.

1st sentence	This is to confirm the meeting arranged for next Thursday, 14 December, at 2.0 p.m.
2nd sentence	Please note that the meeting will be held at Head Office (West Lion Square) and not at the factory.
3rd or closing sentence	I am looking forward to seeing you again and hope that we have a profitable meeting.

4. No complimentary close needed. We will assume that the originator will initial the memorandum.
5. Check draft. Pay especial attention to dates, times and names.
6. Assemble carbon pack and type the memo.
7. Check it.
8. Present it for initialling.
9. Do not apply.
10. Do not apply.
11. Send memorandum to mail room.

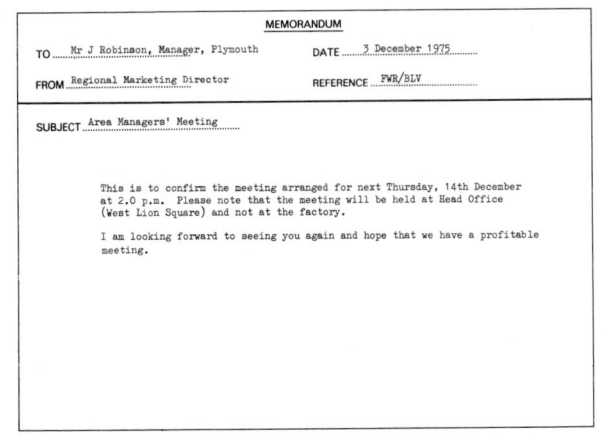

```
                           MEMORANDUM
   TO  Mr J Robinson, Manager, Plymouth    DATE   3 December 1975
   FROM  Regional Marketing Director       REFERENCE  FWR/BLV

   SUBJECT  Area Managers' Meeting


        This is to confirm the meeting arranged for next Thursday, 14th December
        at 2.0 p.m.  Please note that the meeting will be held at Head Office
        (West Lion Square) and not at the factory.
        I am looking forward to seeing you again and hope that we have a profitable
        meeting.
```

The memorandum, typed and initialled.

2 Transmittal letters

Transmittal letters are written to cover the despatch of enclosures or parcels. They are sometimes called *covering letters*. The typist usually adopts some method (such as typing *Enc* at the lower left-hand edge of the letter) to remind the despatch clerk or herself that an enclosure has to be included with the letter.

If a transmittal letter refers to the despatch of a packet or parcel sent separately as a postal package or a parcel, the phrase 'sent under separate cover' is usually included in the letter and followed by the name of the postal or parcel service which has been used, e.g.

```
We have despatched to you today, under separate cover, by registered post, a.

We have sent you today, by goods train, a parcel.....
```

Copies of covering and transmittal letters, whilst not proving that a package was actually sent, are important office records. Certificates of posting or receipts obtained for packages sent under separate cover should be stapled to the copies of covering letters.

```
                    CERTIFICATE OF POSTING
              Unregistered letters and ordinary parcels only

    .................(Number) items entered*     ┌──────────────┐
    overleaf have been posted here today.        │  Postage     │
                                                 │ stamps to the│
    Accepting Officer's Initials.................│  value of 1p │
                                                 │ for each item│
    *Sender should copy the address in full      │ to be affixed│
    overleaf, and the items should be pre-       │   here by    │
    sented in the order in which they are        │   sender     │
    listed.                                      └──────────────┘

    Conditions:—(1) In the event of loss, damage or delay, this certificate
                    will confer no title to compensation.

                (2) Any items in respect of which this certificate is issued
                    will not be checked in the post, or afforded special
                    treatment.
```

Certificates of Posting may be obtained from post offices when letters or parcels are posted. Certificates of Posting for overseas parcels are issued free of charge. A Certificate of Posting for a letter or a packet or an ordinary inland parcel costs 1p.

Instruction

'Would you send this form off to Mrs Swanson, please Nadia? Tell her to complete it and return it as soon as possible.' (Let us assume that the Personnel Manager is talking to Nadia and that in this instance she can sign the letter on his behalf.)

Working steps

1 Make sure that you have Mrs Swanson's full name, initials and address. Note the name of the form as you will want to refer to it in the covering letter.
2 Let us assume that the Rule of the House in the firm is for letters to be displayed in the fully-blocked style.

3 Draft the message.
   As the letter is to a lady, it will start Dear Madam

   1st sentence — I enclose an application form for the post of Assistant Actuary with this firm.

   2nd sentence (No additional information needed)

   Last sentence — Would you please complete the form and return it to me as soon as possible.

4 Complimentary close.
   As the letter started Dear Madam the standard close is Yours faithfully
   Then leave a space before typing the name and designation of the Personnel Manager.
   Remember to type Enc in the lower left-hand corner of the letter to remind you to enclose the application form.
5 Check your draft. Pay special attention to names and addresses.
6 Assemble carbon pack and type the letter.
7 Check it.
8 Sign it yourself and write the letters p.p. at the side of the Personnel Manager's name.

   p.p. stands for per procuriationem and shows that you are authorised to sign on behalf of the Personnel Manager.

9 Select an envelope large enough to take the letter and the application form.
10 Check the enclosure. Fold it carefully with the covering letter. Put them in the envelope and seal it.
11 Arrange for the letter to be stamped or franked and mailed as soon as possible.

3 Letters of confirmation

As implied by the title, letters of confirmation are letters written to confirm arrangements. The arrangements are usually reservations or bookings at hotels or for travel arrangements or tickets. There is nothing particularly difficult about writing letters of confirmation but the recipients usually prefer them to be signed by the originators personally, i.e. a confirmation signed by the person concerned has more validity than one signed 'on behalf of' or 'p.p.'.

Instruction

'Type a short letter to the hotel in Bridlington, please Gillian, to confirm the booking I made by 'phone this morning—a single room with bath for two nights, next Wednesday and Thursday. I'd like to sign the letter before I go to lunch, so will you do it at once, please?' (Assume that Dr. Antony Hirsh is talking to Gillian).

RLT/NB

14 February 1975

Mrs G Swanson
45 The Crescent
EDINBURGH
EH2 3AR

Dear Madam

I enclose an application form for the post of Assistant Actuary with this firm.

Would you please complete the form and return it to me as soon as possible.

Yours faithfully

Nadia Bustani

R L Thorpe
Personnel Manager

Enc

The transmittal letter Nadia composed, typed and signed. Notice that it is typed on A5 paper in the fully-blocked style with open punctuation, i.e. no punctuation marks at all before and after the body of the letter. Notice that Nadia has signed the letter herself and added the letters p.p. to show that she is authorised to sign on behalf of the Personnel Manager.

Working steps
1. Make sure you have the full name and address of the hotel and check the dates for the Wednesday and Thursday concerned. Make a note of the price quoted.

2. Decide how you will display the communication. This is obviously a letter. Let us assume that it is a personal business letter, i.e. it will not be typed on headed letter paper so you will have to type the address of the originator at the top right-hand corner of the page.

3. Draft the letter.

1st sentence	I am writing to confirm ⎫ 　　　　　　　　　　　⎬ our This is to confirm　　⎭ telephone conversation this morning when I reserved a single room with bath for next Wednesday and Thursday, 4th/5th April, at £8.50 per night including breakfast and VAT.
2nd sentence	I shall be travelling from London by car and hope to arrive about 6.0 p.m.
Last sentence	Please acknowledge this booking as soon as possible.

4. Decide how to close the letter. Dr Hirsh will sign it himself.
5. Check the draft. Pay special attention to dates, times and prices and terms, e.g. inclusive of VAT.
6. Select the paper size—we have used 2/3 A4 in this example—collate the carbon pack and feed it into the typewriter. Type the letter.
7. Read through the letter before removing it from the machine and correct any errors.
8. Present the letter for signature.
9. Type an envelope.
10. Check address on envelope against address on letter. Fold letter and insert in envelope. Stamp with correct denomination of stamps for either first class or second class mail.
11. Mail the letter as soon as possible.

4 Acknowledgments
Written acknowledgments may be made by:

1. completing pre-printed postcards or;
2. composing letters.

An example of a pre-printed postcard is shown below. All the typist has to do is to complete the details and type the name and address on the other side of the card.

                                                            Flat 89
                                                            362 Maple Terrace
                                                            COVENTRY CV1 5BD

                                                            30th March 1975

The Manager
Europa Hotel
BRIDLINGTON Yorks
YO16 3RC

Dear Sir

This is to confirm our telephone conversation this morning when I
reserved a single room with bath for next Wednesday and Thursday,
4th/5th April, at £8.50 per night including breakfast and VAT.

I shall be travelling from London by car and hope to arrive about
6.0 p.m.

Please acknowledge this booking as soon as possible.

Yours faithfully

Dr A Hirsh   LRCP MRCS

A letter of confirmation typed on 2/3 A4 paper in the fully-blocked style with open punctuation. The letter is a personal one so the typist has typed the address of the originator at the top right-hand side of the page. As a matter of personal preference and to achieve a balanced display, the date has been typed underneath the originator's address.

Edward Arnold   25 Hill St.,
(Publishers) Ltd.   London W1X 8LL
                         01-493 8511

                                    date ....

We acknowledge receipt of the MS entitled

....

While every care will be taken of the MS we do not hold ourselves responsible for its loss or damage by fire or otherwise.

A pre-printed acknowledgment card.

Acknowledgments may be sent, as in this example, to let the writer know that his letter (or order, or booking, as the case may be) has been received and that he can expect a further communication in due course; or an acknowledgment may be sent, as in the worked example on page 142, to provide a written record of the receipt of an important parcel or document.

Instruction

'The parcel of account books, vouchers, bank statements and so on arrived back from the auditors this morning, Leslie. Just drop them a written acknowledgment, will you please?'·(Assume that the speaker is the Chief Accountant and that the name and address of the auditors is on the covering letter.)

Working steps
1. Compose the reply address from the auditors' covering letter.
2. The communication is obviously a short business letter. You will display it according to the Rule of the House which in this case is semi-indented.
3. Draft the letter.

1st sentence	I thank you for your letter dated 5 June and acknowledge receipt of the parcel containing account books, vouchers, bank statements and other financial records.
2nd or further sentences	Not necessary

4. As the letter started   Dear Sir

    the close will be   Yours faithfully

    followed by four line spaces for the Chief Accountant to sign his name; then you will type his name and underneath that the words

                                  Chief Accountant

5. Check the draft. Pay especial attention to dates, names and addresses.
6. Assemble carbon pack and type the letter. As it is very short you can use A5 paper.
7. Check the letter.
8. Present it for signature.
9. Type an envelope.
10. Check address on envelope against address on letter. Fold and insert signed letter.
11. Arrange for the letter to be stamped or franked and mailed as soon as possible.

FRB/LS   8 June 1975

D B Collins Esq
Messrs Gimson and Quirk
City House
Dominion Square
LONDON EC2 4RA

Dear Mr Collins

    I thank you for your letter dated 5 June and acknowledge receipt of the parcel containing account books, vouchers, bank statements and other financial records.

                        Yours faithfully

                        F R Browning
                        Chief Accountant

Letter of acknowledgment typed on A5 paper in semi-indented style with open punctuation.

EXERCISES

1 Write a letter covering the despatch of a parcel of proofs to an author. The letter will be signed by the Education Editor, who would like the corrected proofs returned as soon as possible.

2 Compose an interoffice communication from the Sales Manager to the Chief Accountant asking him for an analysis of outstanding accounts up to the end of last month.

3 'Would you send off this form to Mr Roberts, please? Ask him to complete it and return it as soon as possible.' The Claims Manager is speaking. The form is an Accident Report form.

4 'Would you please type a letter to the hotel in Weymouth to confirm the booking I made by 'phone this morning—a double room with bath for one week from next Friday. It's going to cost £120, full

board, for two people, including VAT. Mrs Grace Holmes, a solicitor, is speaking. The letter will be sent from her home address.

5 Write a letter acknowledging receipt of a cheque for £500 from the Western Broadcasting Corporation. The letter should be sent to the Manager, Contracts Department. It will be signed by a script-writer Dennis Ferguson.

6 Send an interoffice memorandum from the Works Manager to the Manager of the Travel Department, asking him to book a London/Glasgow flight, an overnight hotel in Glasgow and a return Glasgow/London flight for the Works Manager and his assistant for Monday and Tuesday next.

7 Write a letter to confirm a telephone call to the bank requesting £400 to be transferred from deposit to current account. The letter will be signed by the Chief Accountant. You will need to quote the numbers of both accounts.

8 'Would you write to the artist and acknowledge receipt of these sketches, please? Say that I'll telephone her about them when I get back from Paris at the end of next week.' The Fashion Editor is speaking.

9 Write a letter from the Secretary of the National Women's Organisation to Miss Fiona Maitland confirming a telephone conversation in which Miss Maitland agreed to speak to members of the Organisation at a meeting at 8.0 p.m. on Thursday, 11 November.

10 Write a memorandum from the Personnel Director. Address it to all heads of departments. The subject is 'Promotions Board'. Say that the meeting to discuss the setting up of a new Promotions Board will be held in the Personnel Director's office, Room 104, on Thursday, 10 March, at 14.30 hours. The name of the Personnel Manager is A. Baker.

Glossary 1
Business Terms

TRADING

A/C., account current
ad val., ad valorem
A/R., all risks (marine)
A/S., account sales

B/E., bill of exchange
B/L., bill of lading
B/P., bills payable
B/R., bills receivable

C. & F., cost and freight
carr. fwd., carriage forward
carr. pd., carriage paid
C.B.D., cash before delivery
c.i.f., cost, insurance, freight
c.i.f. & c., cost, insurance, freight and commission
c.i.f. & e., cost, insurance, freight and exchange
c.i.f.i., cost, insurance, freight and interest
cld., cleared
C/R., carrier's risk
c/s., case(s)
C.W.O., cash with order

D/a., days after acceptance; documents against acceptance
D/D., delivered at docks
debs., debentures
D/N., debit note
D/O., delivery order
D/P., documents against payment
D/W., dock warrant

E. & O.E., errors and omissions excepted
E.O.M., end of month following date of sale
Exd., examined
Ex. Int., not including interest

f.a.s., free alongside ship
F/D., free docks
f.f.a., free from alongside
f.o., free overside
f.o.b., free on board
f.o.c., free of charge(s)
f.o.d., free of damage
f.o.r., free on rail
f.o.s., free on steamer
f.o.t., free on truck
f.o.w., free on wagon
Frt., freight
Fwd., forward

G/A., general average
g.r.t., gross registered tonnage

H.M.C., Her Majesty's Customs

I.B.R.D., International Bank for Reconstruction and Development (World Bank)
I.C.A., International Co-operative Administration
I.M.F., International Monetary Fund
ins., insurance
int., interest
in trans., in transit
inv., invoice

J/A., joint account

Lt., long ton

mdse., merchandise
M.I.P., marine insurance policy
M.P., months after payment
M.S., months after sight
M.T., mail transfer

N.E., no effects
N.F., no funds
N/O., no orders
n.o.p., not otherwise provided
n.s., not specified

O/a., on account
O/d., on demand
O/o., order of
O.R., owner's risk

P.A., private account
pcs., pieces
pd., paid
p.f., pro forma
pkgs., packages
P.L., partial loss
pm., premium

R.I., reinsurance

S/a., without date
S.D.B.L., sight draft bill of lading
shipt., shipment
S/N., shipping note
S.O., seller's option
S.T. or S.tn., short ton
Stg., sterling

T.L.O., total loss only
T.T., telegraphic transfer

U/w., underwriters

W.B., way bill
W/M., weight or measurement
W.O.G., with other goods
W/R., warehouse receipt
W/W., warehouse warrant

BANKING

A/c or acct., account

A/C, current account, account giving no interest: money can be withdrawn on demand

At Sight, payable on demand

Bank rate, rate charged by Bank of England for discounting bills

B/D., bank draft

Bk., bank, book

B.N., bank note

B.o., branch office

B.S., balance sheet, statement of assets and liabilities

C/A., capital account

Cert A.I.B., Certificated Associate, Institute of Bankers

Cheque, a written order to a banker to pay a named sum to a named person

Clearing House, where banks exchange money for cheques drawn on one another

C/O, cash order

Credit transfer, method of settling debts with bank as intermediary, by paying amounts straight into creditor's bank (useful to people with no bank account)

Cum div., with dividend

D/A, deposit account, account giving interest, money can be withdrawn only after notice

Devalue, reduce the exchange rate of currency

D/P, documents against payment

Drawer, person who draws cheque upon another; the person who writes the cheque

Endorse, to sign document, especially cheque, on the back

Ex div., without dividend

Fiduciary Issue, issue of banknotes without gold backing

Floaters, Government bonds etc. as securities

Funding, changing short-term to long-term debt

Gilt-edged Securities, securities of the highest class which are easy to cash

Giro system, one run by Post Office and one run by clearing banks for the payment of money by e.g. cheques

Gold Reserve, amount of gold coin and bullion held by the Bank of England or by another country

Hard Currency, any strong currency used as a medium of exchange, e.g. US dollars

H.O., head office

I.M.F., International Monetary Fund

Industrial Bankers, specialists in financing hire-purchase transactions

IOU, I owe you, memorandum of a debt

Issuing House, financial institution concerned with new issues of stocks and shares

J/A, joint account

£, pound

L/C, Letter of credit, authorising a person to draw money in another place, up to a sum specified by the person's bank

Ledger, principal book of accounts, made up at regular intervals

Legal tender, money which creditor is bound to accept in payment

Liquid Asset, quickly converted into cash

Liquidity Ratio, ratio of a banker's liquid assets to liabilities—traditionally kept at over 30 per cent in Britain

Lombard Street, a term often used when referring to the London money market

M/C., marginal credit

M.D., memorandum of deposit

m/d, months after date

Mint, place where money is coined

N/A, no advice, non-acceptance

N/E, n/f, no effects, no funds, written by banker on a dishonoured cheque

Negotiable Instruments, documents which are transferred carrying legal rights to the final holder, such as a bank note or a bill of exchange

Not Negotiable, words on a cheque *warning* that a thief *may* not get a good title

N.P., Notary Public, usually a solicitor, authorised to attest contracts etc. and protest bills of exchange

n.s., not sufficient funds, written by banker on a dishonoured cheque

o/d, on demand

Orders not to pay, written by banker on a dishonoured cheque

Overdraft, authorised drawing from current account in excess of balance

Overdraw, accidental drawing from current account when the balance is nil

P.A., private account

Paper money, all engagements to pay issued

by banks of Government Departments and circulated in place of coin, such as money orders and bank notes

Payee, person or firm to whom a cheque or bill of exchange is made payable

Paying-in slip, paper showing amount paid into a person's account in cash or cheques

P/N, promissory note, signed, written document promising to pay a certain sum to a specified person at a certain time

Realisation Account, especially opened account when a firm is being wound up or sold

Refer to drawer, written by banker on a dishonoured cheque

Securities, document giving the holder the right to property which is not in his possession, such as mortgages, insurance policies, bills of lading, bonds, stocks or shares

Sight Bill, bill of exchange payable when presented

Sovereign, British gold coin of £1 face value

Special deposit, certain amount of Joint Stock Banks' money which must be put into Bank of England during a Credit Squeeze

Statement, document issued to customer showing the state of his current account

Sterling Area, countries which trade in currencies based on the British monetary system now referred to as Scheduled Territories

Stop a cheque, drawer instructs bank in writing not to cash cheque when it is presented

Teller, bank cashier

T.M.O., telegraph money order

Token money, coins of less metallic value than the sum written on them

Travellers' Cheques, written orders drawn upon bank in Britain, paid for in this country, and cashable overseas

Treasury, British Government Department managing public revenue

Treasury Bill, issued by the Treasury to raise money for short periods and sold to the highest bidder

Usance, customary period allowed for payment of bills of exchange between two countries

Wall Street, the address of the New York Stock Exchange

INSURANCE

Accident, an unexpected mishap

Act of God, an event which no human foresight can prevent, e.g. earthquake, but *not* frost damage which can be prevented if precautions are taken

Agent, a person who acts on behalf of another, called the principal

Annuity, annual payment for a specified time or until death

Assignment, transfer of right or property; document making such a transfer

Assurance (or Insurance), see Insurance

Assured (or Insured), see Insured

Assurer (or Insurer), see Insurer

Bond, an undertaking by somebody to pay a sum of money or to do or not do a certain thing

Broker, an intermediary who advises his clients and arranges their insurance

Brokerage, see Commission

Commission, an agent's or broker's remuneration. It is also called brokerage

Cover, a synonym for insure or insurance, or the scope of any insurance, e.g. The cover includes fire

Cover Note, a temporary document proving that cover exists until the issue of the stamped policy

Days of Grace, the period during which the policy is kept in force pending payment of a premium (usually 15 days for monthly premiums and one month for premiums payable quarterly, half-yearly or annually)

Endorsement, amendment or addition to policy, certificate or cover note; the endorsement is attached to the original document

Endowment Assurance, a policy with the sum assured payable on a fixed future date, or at death if the person assured dies before the end of the term. It can be with or without profits

Ex gratia, a payment made voluntarily, where no legal liability exists

Fidelity Bonds, policy guaranteeing fidelity of employees, especially those handling large amounts of money

Good faith, see Utmost good faith

Indemnity, compensation for loss or injury

Insurable interest, a person taking out insurance must have a pecuniary interest in the person or thing insured

Insurance, a contract whereby the insurer undertakes to indemnify another person or to pay that person a sum of money if and when a specified event, such as death, happens

Insured, the policyholder or other person who is indemnified under a policy of insurance

Lloyd's, a Corporation which does no underwriting but provides facilities for its underwriting members who deal with marine and other classes of insurance

Loss, the amount for which the insurer is liable when a claim is made under a policy; event which results in a claim under a policy

Mortgagee, a person who lends money on the security of property

Mortgagor, an owner who borrows money on the security of his property

Premium, the money paid by the insured person to the insurers for the cover to be provided; payable annually, half-yearly, quarterly, monthly or weekly

Proposal form, the form on which a proposal is made to an insurer

Proprietary Office, an Insurance company with shareholders

Risk, the subject of insurance, either a person or thing; a hazard the insurer covers, but not an inevitable happening

Salvage, reward or compensation paid to a person who saves goods at sea from shipwreck or other loss

Subrogation, the right of the insurer to keep an amount up to the claim paid of any money received from others responsible or partly responsible for the loss

Surrender, cancellation of an insurance before the normal time

Surrender value, the sum payable to the insured when a life policy is surrendered

Tariff, a scale of rates adopted in common by a number of companies

Tort, a civil wrong causing injury to a person or his property; the injured party can claim reparation for his loss; not a crime

Underwriter, name given to an insurer who underwrites a risk by accepting liability for a loss

Underwriting, accepting liability for any loss to the person or property insured from an insured hazard

Utmost good faith, the insurer accepts information he is given about the subject of the insurance in good faith; if the information is untrue the insurer may repudiate claims under the policy

With Profits (Participating) Policy, the policy-holder is entitled to share in the profits of the company. Bonuses, which are payable with the sum assured, are usually declared at intervals of one to five years

NOTE For secretaries who are engaged in specialist work, such as the law, medicine or technology, it is recommended that specialised dictionaries are obtained.

Glossary 2
Meeting and Conference Terms

Addendum, an amendment
Adjournment, postponement
Agenda, items of business at a meeting
Amendment, a proposal to change Bill or motion

Block vote, voting by cards, each of which has a specified number of votes
By-election, Parliamentary election between General Elections, to fill a seat vacated for various reasons

Candidate, person thought likely to gain any position
Casting vote, deciding vote, given by Chairman usually
Clause, an item of a Bill
Committee, group appointed to discuss a subject
Communique, official statement to the Press

Data, information
Delegate, elected representative at a conference
Deputation, group appointed to meet or interview others
Division, vote taken on motion or Bill

Erratum, error in printing
Ex officio, by virtue of office
Exhaustive vote, vote by rounds, one candidate being eliminated each time

Facsimile, an exact copy
Filibuster, obstructionist in legislative assembly

'Gagging', stopping from speaking

Heckle, to question severely (usually a Parliamentary candidate)

In camera, in private
Interim report, preliminary report

Journal, daily record; Minute Book of House of Commons

Kangaroo, selection of certain amendments for discussion and exclusion of others

Locus standi, right or authority
Lords spiritual, ecclesiastical members of the House of Lords
Lords temporal, lay members of the House of Lords

Main question, main issue before a meeting
Mandate, an order; instruction given by electors to a Member of Parliament
Mass-meeting, a large assembly of people for some special purpose
Minutes, short summary of the proceedings of a meeting
Motion, a proposition made in a deliberative assembly

Nem. con. (*nemine contradicente*) without opposition
Nem. dis. (*nemine dissentiente*), without dissent
Nominate, to propose a candidate for an office

Omnibus motion, comprehensive motion
Opposition, body of those opposing the existing administration or Government
Orders of the day, Agenda of the House of Commons
Original motion, the first motion on any subject

Peroration, the concluding part of a speech
Pious motion, a motion expressing an opinion only
Poll, number of votes recorded at an election
Preamble, the opening clauses of a statute setting out its object
Precedent, a parallel case in the past
Private meeting, meeting which is closed to the public
Programme of business, agenda
Pro rata, in proportion
Prorogation, termination of Parliamentary meetings
Public meeting, a meeting which is open to the public, wherever it may be held
Put the question, put to the vote, divide the meeting

Question, issue raised by a motion
Questionnaire, a list of questions in an official circular
Quorum, smallest number of members who must be present at a meeting to enable proceedings to be valid

Record vote, a vote taken by a roll call
'Reference back', an amendment by which a report is sent back for further consideration to original body which drafted it
Representative, one who is authorised to act for others
Rescind, repeal, annul
Resolution, formal proposal in a legislative assembly or a public meeting
Résumé, summary
Returning Officer, a local official who presides at an election and declares the result
Rhetoric, the art of speaking eloquently
Rostrum, platform used for public speaking

Schedule, appendix to a larger document or Act
Scrutineer, a person who supervises the voting at an election
Secretariat, department of the Secretary of an organisation
Section, division or sub-division of a Statute
Select Committee, body of Members specially selected by Parliament
Session, sitting or assembling of a legislative body; the time between the first sitting and the adjournment of Parliament
Speaker, Chairman of the House of Commons
Standing Orders, rules stating the way in which a meeting shall be conducted

Teller, member appointed to count votes on a division
Terms of Reference, words laying down powers of a special committee

Ultra vires, beyond the powers or rights possessed

Verbatim, word for word
Veto, authoritative prohibition
Vice-Chairman, a substitute chairman
Viva-voce, spoken: orally

White Paper, a Government report, so named because of its white cover

Glossary 3

Abbreviations and Initials in Common Use

It is becoming increasingly common to print and type abbreviations without full stops, particularly in the case of acronyms such as NATO and UNESCO

a, ampere
A.1, first class
A/A, articles of association
A.A., Automobile Association; Associate in Arts; Associate in Accounting
A.B., able-bodied seaman
A.B.A., Amateur Boxing Association
abbr., abbrev., abbreviation
abr., abridge; abridgment
A.C., Alpine Club; alternating current
a/c, account; account current
A.C.A., Associate of the Institute of Chartered Accountants
A.C.G.I., Associate of City and Guilds Institute
A.C.I.S., Associate of the Chartered Institute of Secretaries
A.D., *anno domini*, in the year of our Lord
A.D.C., *aide-de-camp*
ad fin., *ad finem*, at, to the end

A.E.C., Atomic Energy Commission; Association of Education Committees
ad lib., *ad libitum*, at pleasure
ad loc., *ad locum*, at this place
Adm., Admiral; Admiralty; administrator
ad val., *ad valorem*, according to the value
advt., advertisement
A.E.R.E., Atomic Energy Research Establishment
A.E.U., Amalgamated Engineering Union
A.F.A., Amateur Football Association
A.F.C., Air Force Cross
A.F.M., Air Force Medal
A.-G., Attorney-General
Ag., *argentum*, silver
agric., agricultur(e) -al
A.G.S.M., Associate of the Guildhall School of Music
agt., agent; agreement
A.I., artificial insemination
A.I.C., Associate of the Institute of Chemistry of Great Britain and Ireland
A.I.C.E., Associate of the Institution of Civil Engineers
A.I.Mech.E., Associate of the Institution of Mechanical Engineers
A.L.C.M., Associate of the London College of Music
Ald., Alderman
a.m., *ante meridiem*, before noon
A.M.I.Chem.E., Associate Member of the Institution of Chemical Engineers
A.M.I.E.E., Associate Member of the Institution of Electrical Engineers
A.M.I.Mech.E., Associate Member of the Institution of Mechanical Engineers
amt., amount
anon., anonymous
A.O.D., Ancient Order of

Druids; Army Ordnance Department
A.P., Associated Press
ap., *apud,* according to
app., appendix; appointed; apprentice
A.R.A., Associate of the Royal Academy
A.R.A.M., Associate of the Royal Academy of Music
A.R.C.A., Associate of the Royal College of Art
A.R.B.A., Associate of the Royal Society of British Artists
archit., architecture
A.R.C.M., Associate of the Royal College of Music
A.R.I.B.A., Associate of the Royal Institute of British Architects
A.R.I.C., Associate of the Royal Institute of Chemistry
A.S.A., Amateur Swimming Association; Atomic Scientists' Association

B.A., Bachelor of Arts; British Airways
B.A.C.I.E., British Association for Commercial and Industrial Education
B.A.O.R., British Army of the Rhine
B.B., Boys' Brigade; double black (lead pencils)
B.B.C., British Broadcasting Corporation
B.C., Before Christ; British Columbia
B.Ch., *Baccalaureus Chiurgiae,* Bachelor of Surgery
B.D., Bachelor of Divinity
B.E.A., British European Airways
B.E.M., British Empire Medal
B.I.F., British Industries Fair
B.I.M., British Institute of Management
B.I.R., Board of Inland Revenue
B.L., Bachelor of Laws; Bachelor of Letters; British Legion
B.M., Bachelor of Medicine; British Museum
B.M.A., British Medical Association
B.M.J., British Medical Journal
B.O.A.C., British Overseas Airways Corporation
B.R., British Rail
B.S., Bachelor of Science; Bachelor of Surgery; British Standard; balance sheet; bill of sale
B.Sc., Bachelor of Science
B.S.I., British Standards Institution
B.S.T., British Summer Time
Bt., Baronet
B.T., Board of Trade; Board of Treasury
B.T.U., British thermal unit
B.U.P., British United Press

C., centigrade
cat., catalogue
C.B.E., Commander of the Order of the British Empire
C.C., County Council
C.E., Civil Engineer
cf., compare
chq., cheque
C.I.D., Criminal Investigation department
cm, centimetre
CN, credit note; circular note
C.N.D., Campaign for Nuclear Disarmament
Co., Company; county
c/o, care of
C.O.D., cash on delivery
C. of E., Church of England
C.o.I.D., Council of Industrial Design
Co-op., Co-operative Society
C.R.O., Criminal Records Office
C.U., Cambridge University
cwt., hundredweight

d.b., Day Book
D.B.E., Dame Commander of the Order of the British Empire
d.c., direct current
D.C.L., Doctor of Civil Law
D.D., Doctor of Divinity
D/D, demand draft
def., deferred
deg., degree
dept., department
D.E.S., Department of Education and Science
dft., draft
dis., discount
dist., district
div., division
D.Lit(t)., Doctor of Literature (Letters)
D.M., Doctor of Medicine; Doctor of Music
do., ditto
doz., dozen
Dr., debtor; doctor; director
dr., drachma; dram
D.S.C., Distinguished Service Cross
D.S(c)., Doctor of Science
D.V., God willing *(deo volente)*

Ed., edition; editor
e.e., errors excepted
E.F.T.A., European Free Trade Association
e.g., for example
e. & o.e., errors and omissions excepted
Esq., Esquire
etc., and so forth *(et cetera)*
E.T.U., Electrical Trades Union
ex., examined; out of; without

F., Fahrenheit
F.A., Football Association; Faculty of Actuaries
F.B.A., Fellow of the British Academy
F.C.A., Fellow of the Institue of Chartered Accountants
F.C.I.S., Fellow of the Chartered Institute of Secretaries
F.C.P., Fellow of the College of Preceptors

151

F.M., Field Marshal
F.O., firm offer; Flying Officer; Field Officer; Foreign Office
F.P.A., Family Planning Association; Foreign Press Association
F.R.A.M., Fellow of the Royal Academy of Music
F.R.A.S., Fellow of the Royal Astronomical Society
F.R.C.M., Fellow of the Royal College of Music
F.R.C.P., Fellow of the Royal College of Physicians
F.R.C.S., Fellow of the Royal College of Surgeons
F.R.G.S., Fellow of the Royal Geographical Society
F.R.I.B.A., Fellow of the Royal Institute of British Architects
F.R.I.C.S., Fellow of the Royal Institution of Chartered Surveyors
F.R.S., Fellow of the Royal Society
F.R.S.M., Fellow of the Royal Society of Medicine
ft., feet; foot
F.Z.S., Fellow of the Zoological Society

g., gauge; gramme
gal., gallon(s)
G.B., Great Britain
Gen., General
G.H.Q., General Headquarters
G.L.C., Greater London Council
G.M.C., General Medical Council
G.M.T., Greenwich Mean Time
G.N.P., Gross National Product
G.P., general practitioner
G.P.O., General Post office
gr., grain; grammar
gr wt., gross weight
gym., gymnasium; gymnastics

H.E., His Eminence; His Excellency
H.H., His (Her) Highness; His Holiness
H.M.I., His (Her) Majesty's Inspector
H.M.S.O., His (Her) Majesty's Stationery Office
H.P., high pressure; hire purchase; House Physician
H.Q., Headquarters
H.T., high tension
H.W.M., High Water Mark

i/c., in charge
I.C.I., Imperial Chemical Industries
I.L.E.A., Inner London Education Authority
i.e., that is *(id est)*
I.L.O., International Labour Office
I.L.P., Independent Labour Party
in., inch; inches
Inc., Incorporated
init., in the beginning *(in initio)*
I.N.R.I., *Jesus Nazarenus, Rex Judaeorum* (Jesus of Nazareth, King of the Jews)
I.O.M., Isle of Man
I.R.A., Irish Republican Army
I.R.O., Inland Revenue Office
I.S.O., International Organisation for Standardisation
iss., issue
I.T.B., Industrial Training Board
I.W. or **I.o.W.**, Isle of Wight

J.A., Judge Advocate
J.P., Justice of the Peace
jr., junior
junc., junction

K.B., King's Bench; Knight Bachelor; Knight of the Order of the Bath
K.B.E., Knight Commander of the Order of the British Empire
K.C., King's College; King's Council; Knight(s) of Columbus
K.C.B., Knight Commander of the Order of the Bath
K.C.M.G., Knight Commander St. Michael and St. George
K.C.V.O., Knight Commander of the Royal Victorian Order
K.G., Knight of the Order of the Garter
kg, kilogramme
km, kilometre
k.-o., knock-out
K.T., Knight of the Thistle
kw, kilowatt

L, Latin; learner (on motor vehicle)
Lab., Labour; Labrador
L.A.C., Leading Aircraftman; London Athletic Club
lb, pound (weight)
L.C., Lord Chancellor; Lord Chamberlain
L.C.J., Lord Chief Justice
L.C.P., Licentiate of the College of Preceptors
L.D.S., Licentiate of Dental Surgery
Litt.D., Doctors of Letters
LL.B., Bachelor of Laws
LL.D., Doctors of Laws
LL.M., Master of Laws
L.R.A.M., Licentiate of the Royal Academy of Music
L.R.C.P., Licentiate of the Royal College of Physicians
L.R.C.S., Licentiate of the Royal College of Surgeons
L.R.C.V.S., Licentiate of the Royal College of Veterinary Surgeons
L.T.A., Lawn Tennis Association; London Teachers Association
Ltd., Limited
L.T.E., London Transport Executive
L.W.M., Low Water Mark

m, metre

M.A., Master of Arts
M.B., Bachelor of Medicine
M.B.E., Member of the Order of the British Empire
M.C., Military Cross; Master of Ceremonies
M.C.C., Marylebone Cricket Club
M.Ch., Master of Surgery
M.C.P., Member of the College of Preceptors
M.D., Doctor of Medicine
M.D.S., Master in Dental Surgery
M.E., Mining Engineer; Middle English
memo, memorandum
M.F.H., Master of Foxhounds
M.I.C.E., Member of the Institution of Civil Engineers
M.I.C.R., Magnetic ink character recognition
M.I.E.E., Member of the Institution of Electrical Engineers
M.I.Mech.E., Member of the Institution of Mechanical Engineers
min, minute
M.J.I., Member of the Institute of Journalists
M.M., Military Medal
M.O., Medical Officer; money order
M.O.H., Medical Officer of Health
M.P., Member of Parliament
M.P.S., Member of the Pharmaceutical Society
M.R., Master of the Rolls
M.R.C., Medical Research Council
M.R.C.P., Member of the Royal College of Physicians
M.R.C.S., Member of the Royal College of Surgeons
M.R.C.V.S., Member of the Royal College of Veterinary Surgeons
ms(s), Manuscripts(s)
M.Sc., Master of Science
M.S.I.A., Member of the Society of Industrial Artists
Mus.B., Bachelor of Music
M.V.O., Member of the Victorian Order

N.A., North America
N.A.L.G.O., National Association of Local Government Officers
N.A.T.O., North Atlantic Treaty Organisation
N.B., *nota bene* (note well)
N.C.V., no commercial value
N.F.U., National Farmers Union
nom., nominal
N.O.O., not on original
N.P., Notary Public
N.P.L., National Physical Laboratory
N.S., Nova Scotia; Newspaper Society
N.S.P.C.C., National Society for the Prevention of Cruelty to Children
N.T., New Testament
nt.wt., net weight
N.U.J., National Union of Journalists
N.U.R., National Union of Railwaymen
N.U.T., National Union of Teachers
N.Y., New York
N.Z., New Zealand

O.B.E., Order of the British Empire
O.C.R., Optical Character Recognition
O.E., Old English
O.H.M.S., On His (Her) Majesty's Service
O.K., all correct (slang abbreviation)
O.M., Order of Merit
O.R., Official Receiver; other ranks
O.T., Old Testament
O.U., Oxford University
Oxon., of Oxford
oz, ounce, ounces

p., per; page
p.a., by the year *(per annum)*
par., paragraph; parallel
P.C., Privy Council; police constable; post-card
p.c.b., Petty Cash Book
Per pro. or **p.p.,** on behalf of
P.E.R.T., Programme Evaluation and Review Technique
Pf., pfennig (German coin)
Ph.D., Doctor of Philosophy
P.L., profit and loss
P.L.A., Port of London Authority
p.m., after mid-day *(post meridiem)*
P.M.G., Postmaster-General
P.O., Petty Officer; Post Office; postal order
pp., pages; see per pro above
pr., pair
P.R.A., President of the Royal Academy
pro and con, for and against
pro tem., for the time being
P.R.S., President of the Royal Society
P.S., postscript; Privy Seal
pt., pint; point
P.T.A., Parent-Teacher Association
P.T.O., please turn over

Q.C., Queen's Counsel
Q.E.D., which was to be demonstrated *(quod erat demonstrandum)*
Q.M.G., Quartermaster General
Q.M.S., Quartermaster Sergeant
qr., quarter; quire
Q.S., Quarter-Sessions; Queen's Scholar
q.v., which see *(quod vide)*

R.A., Royal Academy; Royal Artillery; Rear-Admiral
R.A.C., Royal Armoured Corps; Royal Automobile Club
R.A.D.A., Royal Academy of Dramatic Art

R.A.F., Royal Air Force
R.A.M., Royal Academy of Music
R.A.M.C., Royal Army Medical Corps
R.A.O.C., Royal Army Ordnance Corps
R.A.S., Royal Astronomical Society; Royal Asiatic Society
R.B., Rifle Brigade
R.B.A., Royal Society of British Artists
R.C., Red Cross; Roman Catholic
R.C.P., Royal College of Physicians
R.C.S., Royal College of Surgeons
R.D., Royal Dragoons; Rural Dean
R.D.C., Rural District Council
re, with reference to
R.E., Right Excellent; Royal Engineers; Royal Exchange
ref., reference
regd., registered
R.G.S., Royal Geographical Society
R.H.S., Royal Humane Society; Royal Horticultural Society
R.I.B.A., Royal Institute of British Architects
R.I.P., rest in peace *(requiescat in pace)*
R.L.S.S., Royal Life Saving Society
Rly., Railway
R.M., Royal Mail; Royal Marines; Resident Magistrate
R.M.A., Royal Marine Artillery; Royal Military Academy (Sandhurst)
R.M.S., Royal Mail Service; Royal Mail Steamer; Royal Microscopical Society
R.N., Royal Navy
R.N.R., Royal Naval Reserve
R.N.V.R., Royal Naval Volunteer Reserve
R.P.M., revolutions per minute
R.S., Royal Society

R.S.A., Royal Scottish Academy; Royal Society of Arts
R.S.P.C.A., Royal Society for the Prevention of Cruelty to Animals
R.S.V.P., reply please *(répondez, s'il vous plaît)*
R.T.C., Royal Tank Corps
Rt. Rev., Right Reverend
R.T.S.A., Retail Trading Standards Association
R.F.U., Rugby Football Union
R.V., Revised Version (bible); Rifle Volunteers
R.Y.S., Royal Yacht Squadron

S.A., South Africa; South America; Salvation Army; subject to approval
S.C.F., Save the Children Fund
S.C.J., Supreme Court of Judicature
s.d., indefinitely *(sine die)*
S.D.F., Social Democratic Federation
S.E., Stock Exchange
S.E.A.T.O., South East Asia Treaty Organisation
S.G., Solicitor-General
S.I. units, Système International D'Unités (International System of Metric Units)
S.M., Short Metre; Senior Magistrate
S.O., Sub-Office
Soc., Society
S.P.C.K., Society for Promoting Christian Knowledge
S.P.G., Society for the Propagation of the Gospel in Foreign Parts
s./s., same size
S.S., Secretary of State; Straits Settlements; Sunday School; steamship
St., Saint; street
st, stone (weight)
stk., stock
supt., superintendent
S.W.G., standard wire gauge

T.A., Territorial Army
T.B., Trial Balance; tuberculosis
T.G.W.U., Transport and General Workers Union
T.N.T., trinitrotoluene (dynamite)
T.O., Telegraph Office; turn over
Treas., Treasurer; Treasury
T.R.H., Their Royal Highnesses
T.T., telegraphic transfers; tuberculin tested (milk)
T.U.C., Trades Union Congress

U.C., University College
U.D.C., Urban District Council; Union of Democratic Control
U.F.C., United Free Church of Scotland
U.K., United Kingdom
Ult., last *(ultimo)*
U.N., United Nations
U.N.A., United Nations Association of Great Britain and Northern Ireland
U.N.I.C.E.F., United Nations Children's Fund
U.N.O., United Nations Organisation
U.S.A., United States of America
U.S.S.R., Union of Soviet Socialist Republics

v., versus; volt
V.A., Vice-Admiral
V. & A., Order of Victoria and Albert
V.A.D., Voluntary Aid Detachment
V.A.T., Value Added Tax
V.C., Vice-Consul; Victoria Cross
V.D., Volunteer Decoration
V.H.F., very high frequency
via, by way of
viz., namely *(videlicet)*
vol., volume; volunteer
V.P., Vice-President
V.S., Veterinary Surgeon

V.T.R., Video Tape Recording (Systems)

W.A., Western Australia; West Africa
W.D., War Department; Works Department
W.E.A., Workers' Educational Association
whf., wharf
W.H.O., World Health Organisation

Whse., warehouse
W.I., West Indies; Women's Institute
wk., week
W.O., War Office; Warrant Officer
W.S., Writer to the Signet

x.c., ex coupon
x.d., ex dividend
x.in., ex interest

Y.B., Year Book
yd., yard
Y.H.A., Youth Hostels Association
Y.M.C.A., Young Men's Christian Association
Y.W.C.A., Young Women's Christian Association

Z.G., Zoological Garden

Glossary 4
Foreign Words and Phrases in Common Use

ab absurdo (L), from absurdity
ab initio (L), from the beginning
á bon marché (F), cheap; a bargain
ab origine (L), from the origin
ad extremum (L), at last; to the extremity
ad hoc (L), for this (special) purpose
ad infinitum (L), to infinity; without limit or end
ad interim (L), for the meanwhile
ad libitum (L), (abb. *ad lib.*), at pleasure
ad nauseam (L), to produce a feeling of disgust
ad referendum (L), to be further considered
ad rem (L), to the thing; to the point; to the purpose
ad valorem (L), (abbr. *ad val.*), according to the value
a fortiori (L), with stronger reason
aide-de-camp (F), (pl. **aides-**) (abbr. A.D.C.), a help; associate; officer attendant on a general

à la (F), in the style of
à la carte (F), selected from the bill of fare
à la française (F), in the French manner
à la lettre (F), word for word; literally
à la mode (F), according to fashion
al fresco (It), in the open air
alma mater (L), foster mother—generally applied to a university
alter ego (L), another self
amour-propre (F), vanity; self-esteem
anno domini (L), in the year of our Lord
ante meridiem (L), (abbr. *a.m.*), before noon
à peu près (F), nearly
a posteriori (L), from the effect to the cause
a priori (L), from the cause to the effect
aqua (L), water
à quoi bon? (F), what's the good?
arrière-pensée (F), mental reservation; afterthought
au courant (F), acquainted with, conversant

au fait (F), expert; well instructed in
au naturel (F), in the natural state
au pair (F), board and lodging without payment, in exchange for some work
au revoir (F), till we meet again; goodbye
à votre santé (F), to your health
beau monde (F), the world of fashion
bête noire (F), pet aversion
bientôt (F), soon
billet doux (F), love letter
bona fide (L), in good faith
bonhomie (F), good nature
bonjour (F), good day; hello
bon mot (F), (pl. **bons mots**), a witticism
bon ton (F), the height of fashion
bon vivant (F), one who lives well
bon voyage (F), a good voyage or journey!
bourgeois (F) (fem. **bourgeoise;** pl. **bourgeoisie**), one of the middle class

carte blanche (F), full powers
cause célèbre (F), a famous case
caveat emptor (L), let the buyer beware
chacun à son goût (F), everyone to his taste
chargé d'affaires (F), person entrusted with state affairs at a foreign court
chef-d'œuvre (F), a masterpiece
cherchez la femme (F), look for the woman in the case
chez moi (F), at (my) home
circa (L), about
coiffeur (F), hairdresser
coiffure (F), hair style
comme ci, comme ça (F), so-so
comme il faut (F), in good taste
communiqué (F), an official communication
compos mentis (L), of sound mind
compte rendu (F), an account rendered, a report
condominium (L), joint rule or sovereignty
confrère (F), a colleague
coram (L), in the presence of
cordon bleu (F), (lit. blue ribbon), a first-class cook
corps diplomatique (F), the diplomatic body
corpus delicti (L), the whole body or nature of the offence
coup d'état (F), a sudden stroke of policy or violence in state affairs
coup de grâce (F), a finishing stroke
crème de la crème (F), the very best; the cream
cui bono? (L), whom does it benefit?
cul-de-sac (F), a street or lane with no outlet
cum grano salis (L), with a grain of salt

d'accord (F), agreed
d'aujourd'hui en huit (F), this day week
de facto (L), in fact; in reality
dégagé (F), free; unrestrained
de jure (L), by right in law
de novo (L), afresh
de profundis (L), from the depths
dérangé (F), disturbed; unwell
de regle (F), customary
de rigueur (F), compulsory; indispensible
desideratum (L), a thing desired; much wanted
détente (F), a relaxing; relief from diplomatic tension
de trop (F), something too much
dies non (L), a day when legal proceedings cannot be taken
Dieu et mon droit (F), God and my right (motto of English sovereigns)
distrait (F), absent-minded
double entente (F), a double meaning
dramatis personae (L), characters of the drama

élan (F), vigour, impetuosity
emeritus (L), title of honour, e.g. professor emeritus; retired from duty but retaining honorary rank
émigré (F), emigrant
en bloc (F), in the lump
en famille (F), among the family; unceremoniously
enfant terrible (F) (lit. an awful child), an embarrassing or uncontrollable person
en masse (F), in a body
en passant (F), in passing, by the way
en rapport (F), in touch; well versed in a subject
en route (F), on the way
entourage (F), surroundings, staff attendants
entrepôt (F), a warehouse
ergo (L), therefore
erratum (L) (pl. errata), error, mistake—in printing or writing
esprit de corps (F), corporate feeling
et cetera (L) (abbr. etc.), and so forth; and the rest
et sequentia (L) (abbr. *et seq.*) and what follows
ex cathedra (L), with authority, from the chair
excelsior (L), higher
exeunt omnes (L), all retire, leave
ex officio (L), by virtue of office
ex parte (L), on one side only
ex post facto (L), restrospective
extra muros (L), beyond the walls

façon de parler (F), manner of speaking
factotum (L), a do-all; general agent, servant or deputy
fait accompli (F), an accomplished fact, something already done
faute de mieux (F), for want of something better
faux pas (F), a false step, a blunder
fiat (L), let it be done; a peremptory order
flagrante delicto (L), in the very act; in the commission of a crime; red-handed
force majeure (F), superior force; the right of the stronger

garçon (F), boy, waiter
gauche (F), left, clumsy
gendarme (F), policeman
gendarmerie (F), police force
genre (F), kind, type
genus (L) (pl. **genera**), type; kind
gourmand (F), glutton
gourmet (F), connoisseur of food and wine
goût (F), taste

habeas corpus (L) (abbr.

hab. corp.) (lit. you may have the body), writ to deliver a person from imprisonment
habitué (F), a frequent visitor of a place
hara-kiri (Jap), suicide
hoi polloi (Gk), the multitude
honi soit qui mal y pense (F), evil be to him who evil thinks
hors de combat (F), out of condition to fight
hôtel de ville (F), town hall

ibidem (L), in the same place
ich dien (G), I serve (motto of the Prince of Wales)
idée fixe (F), a fixed idea
idem (L), the same, or as mentioned before
id est (L), (abbr. *i.e.*) that is
impasse (F), an insurmountable difficulty
in camera (L), in private
in extenso (L), in full (without abridgement)
infra dignitatem (L) (abbr. *infra dig.*), beneath one's dignity
in perpetuum (L), for ever
in re (L), in the matter of
in situ (L), in position
inter alia (L), among other things
interim (L), in the mean time
in toto (L), entirely
in vino veritas (L), truth comes out under the influence of wine
ipse dixit (L), dogmatic assertion
ipso facto (L), by the fact itself, obvious from the facts of the case

jus gentium (L), the law of nations

laissez-faire (F), to let things alone to take their own course; a policy of non-interference
lapsus linguae (L), slip of the tongue
lèse-majesté (F), insulting

the throne; treason
libretto (It), words of a musical work. Writer—librettist
loco citato (L), (abbr. *loc. cit.*), at the place or passage quoted
locum tenens (L), a deputy or substitute
locus standi (L), right to appear before a court

maestro (It), master, composer
magnum opus (L), a great work
maître d'hôtel (F), restaurant manager
mala fide (L), in bad faith
mal de mer (F), sea sickness
mariage de convenance (F), a prudent marriage
ménage (F), household, housekeeping
mille (F), a thousand
minutiae (L), the smallest details
mirabile dictu (L), wonderful to be told
mise en scène (F), manner in which a drama is put on stage; scenic effects
modus operandi (L), manner of working
modus vivendi (L), method of living
multum in parvo (L), much in little
mutatis mutandis (L), necessary changes being made

né, née (F), born
nemine contradicente (L) (abbr. *nem. con.*) without opposition
nemine dissentiente (L) (abbr. *nem. diss.*), without dissent
noblesse oblige (F), noble persons should act nobly
nom de guerre (F), an assumed name
nom de plume (F), pen-name
nonchalance (F), carelessness; indifference
non compos mentis (L), not

of sound mind
non sequitur (L) (abbr. *non seq.*), it does not follow logically
nota bene (L) (abbr. N.B.), mark well
nulli secundus (L), second to none

obiter dictum (L) (pl. **obiter dicta**), a thing said by the way
opus (L), a work
opus citatum (L) (abbr. *op. cit.*), the work cited
outré (F), extravagant

par excellence (F), eminently
pari passu (L), side by side
parvenu (F), one newly risen in position or wealth
passe-partout (F), a master key
pension (F), boarding house
per annum (L), by the year
per capita (L), by the head; individually
per diem (L), by the day
per procurationem (L) (abbr. *per pro.*), on behalf of
per se (L), by itself
persona grata (L), a favoured person
persona non grata (L), a person out of favour
piazza (It), public open square
pièce de résistance (F), the principal dish
pied-à-terre (F), a temporary lodging or resting place
piquant (F), pointed; pungent
pis aller (F), the last resort
a poco a poco (It), little by little
post mortem (L), after death; an examination of a corpse
poste restante (F), place at the Post Office where letters can be addressed to remain until called for
post meridiem (L), (abbr.

p.m.), after noon
précis (F), a summary
prima donna (It) (pl. **prime donne**) leading lady, operatic singer
prima facie (L), at first sight
primus inter pares (L), first among his equals
pro bono publico (L), for the public good
pro et con (L), for and against
pro forma (L), for the sake of form, a formality
pro rata (L), in proportion
pro tempore (L) (abbr. *pro tem.*), for the time being

quasi (L), as if
quid pro quo (L), one thing for another; tit for tat
quod erat demonstrandum (L) (abbr. Q.E.D.), which was to be proved
quod vide (L), (abbr. q.v.), which see

raison d'être (F), reason for existence
rapprochement (F), reconciliation
reductio ad absurdum (L), reducing an argument to an absurdity
répondez, s'il vous plaît (F) (abbr. R.S.V.P.), reply, if you please

résumé (F), a summary
sang-froid (F), cold blood; indifference; apathy
sans souci (F), without care, free and easy
savant (F), a man of learning
savoir faire (F), ability; skill; wits
sine die (L), without appointing a day; adjournment for an indefinite period
sine qua non (L), an indisputable condition
soi-disant (F), self-styled; would-be
soirée (F), an evening party
sotto voce (It), in an undertone
status quo (L), as things stand or stood
stet (L), let it stand
sub judice (L), under consideration by the courts
sub poena (L), under a penalty
sub rosa (L), secretly
supra (L), above

table d'hôte (F), (pl. **tables d'hôte**), ordinary
tant mieux (F), so much the better
tant pis (P), so much the worse

tempus fugit (L), time flies
terra firma (L), solid earth
terra incognita (L), an unknown country
tête-à-tête (F), face to face; a private conversation

ubique (L), everywhere
ultra vires (L), in excess of legal rights
una voce (L), with one voice; unanimously

verbatim et literatim (L), word for word, and letter for letter
via media (L), a middle course
vice versa (L), the reverse
videlicet (L) (abbr. viz.), namely
visa (F), an endorsement on a passport
vis-à-vis (F), opposite; face to face
viva voce (L), by or with the voice; orally
volte-face (F), about-turn: change of attitude
vox populi (L), the voice of the people; public opinion

wagon-lit (F), sleeping car

Glossary 5
Foreign Currencies

COUNTRY	unit	country	unit
Afghanistan	Afghani	Jamaica	£
Albania	Lek	Japan	Yen
Argentina	Peso	Jordan	Dinar
Austria	Schilling	Korea	Won
Australia	£ Australian	Kuwait	Dinar
Belgium	Franc	Lebanon	Pound (Livre)
Bolivia	Boliviano	Liberia	U.S.A. $
Brazil	Cruzeiro	Libya	£
Bulgaria	Leva	Luxembourg	Franc
Burma	Kyat	Malaya	Mal. $
Cambodia	Riel	Mexico	Peso
Canada	Dollar	Nepal	Rupee
Ceylon	Rupee	New Zealand	£ New Zealand
Chile	Escudo	Nicaragua	Cordoba
China	Dollar (People's Bank)	N.W. Indies	Florin
		Norway	Krone
Colombia	Peso	Germany	D/Mark
Congolese Republic	Franc	Ghana	Cedi
		Greece	Drachma
Costa Rica	Colon	Guatemala	Quetzal
Cuba	Peso	Haiti	Gourde
Curacao	Florin	Holland	Florin (Guilder)
Cyprus	Pound	Honduras	Lempira
Czechoslovakia	Crown (Kc.)	Hong Kong	Dollar
Denmark	Krone	Hungary	Florint
Dominican Republic	Peso	Iceland	Krona
		India	Rupee
Ecuador	Sucre	Indonesia	Rupiah
Egypt	Piastre or £ Egyptian	Iran	Rial
		Iraq	Dinar (1,000 Fils)
Eire—see Ireland		Ireland	£
Ethiopia	Dollar	Israel	£ Israeli (1,000 Agurot)
Finland	Markka, Mark		
France	Franc	Italy	Lira

Pakistan	Rupee	Surinam	Gulden
Panama	Balboa	Sweden	Krona
Paraguay	Guarani	Switzerland	Franc
Persia	Rial	Syria and	£ Syrian or
Peru	Sol	Lebanon	£ Lebanese
Philippine Is.	Peso	Thailand	Baht
Poland	Zloty	Tunisia	Dinar
Portugal	Escudo	Turkey	£ Turkish & Lira
Rhodesia and		U.A.R.—see	
Nyasaland	£ Rhodesian	Egypt	
Rumania	Leu	U.S.A.	Dollar
Salvador	Colon	U.S.S.R.	Rouble
Saudi Arabia	Riyal	Uruguay	Peso
Siam	Tical or Baht	Venezuela	Bolivar
Singapore	Dollar	Vietnam	Piastre
South Africa	Rand	West Indies	Dollar
Spain	Peseta	Yugoslavia	Dinar
Sudan	£ Sud.		

Glossary 6

Roman Numerals

1	I	30	XXX
2	II	40	XL
3	III	50	L
4	IV	60	LX
5	V	70	LXX
6	VI	80	LXXX
7	VII	90	XC
8	VIII	100	C
9	IX	200	CC
10	X	300	CCC
11	XI	400	CD
12	XII	500	D
13	XIII	600	DC
14	XIV	700	DCC
15	XV	800	DCCC
16	XVI	900	CM
17	XVII	1000	M
18	XVIII	1500	MD
19	XIX	1900	MCM
20	XX	2000	MM